MICHAEL,

Many Thanks

for coming to our

Long Island

Seminar

Dan

3-17-99

D1563692

HOW TO

DISINHERIT

YOUR

SON-IN-LAW

How to DISINHERIT Your SON-IN-LAW...

...and STIFF THE IRS

Keep <u>Your</u> Money In <u>Your</u> Family

by J. Dan Recer

American Fund Raising Institute ® recognizes the importance of preserving good books. Therefore, it is our policy to have these books published in the United States and printed on acid-free paper.

American Fund Raising Institute ®
Publishing Division
800.496.2370

Although the authors and publisher have exhaustively researched all sources to ensure the accuracy and completeness of the information contained in this book, we assume no responsibility for errors, inaccuracies, omissions or any other inconsistency herein. Any slights against people or organizations are unintentional. Readers should consult an attorney, accountant, financial institution or personal advisor for specific applications to their individual estate planning needs.

98   1
_____

Recer, J. Dan 1936-
      How to Disinherit Your Son-in-Law...and Stiff the IRS; Keep Your Money In Your Family
      / J. Dan Recer

      ISBN   0-9639846-2-4
      LCCN 97-74614

Printed by: Quebecor Printing
Special Effort by: William L. Doyle, Henry A. Niven, Georgia VanDruff
First Edition
Library of Congress Cataloging-in-Publication Data

ACKNOWLEDGMENTS

I am deeply indebted to the scores of bank and non-profit officials who have sponsored our seminars. In the process, they have given me the opportunity to hear and respond to thousands of seminar questions. In addition, they have enabled me to meet privately with, to listen to ... and to make recommendations for ... thousands of families in personal estate planning sessions.

My colleagues, Henry Niven and Georgia VanDruff, have contributed hundreds of hours of careful and meticulous professional assistance in the production of this manuscript.

My friend, Bill Doyle, of North Little Rock, Arkansas, has been both a writing and a publishing mentor.

JDR

Oakton, VA
June, 1997

"In this book, I am going to explain the problems to you, and show you how to design a plan that will disinhert your son-in-law ... and stiff the IRS."

- Dan Recer

DEDICATION

To my mother

"Our son-in-law wished my husband dead so he could get his hands on our farm."

- D.C., Baltimore, MD

"Strangers now live on the corner of my farm that I gave my daughter for a wedding present."

- C.S., Washington, DC

"My ex-son-in-law pocketed the money for which I worked all my life."

- J.B., Atlanta, GA

"I thought we were protected by the premarital agreement; but we lost half of our gift to our daughter."

- D.V., Los Angeles, CA

"When my son-in-law took bankruptcy, his creditors came after my bank account because my daughter's name was on the account."

- L.B., Fayetteville, AR

"I want to be sure my ex-husband does not get his hands on the money I leave my children."

- A.M., Detroit, MI

"When my mother left me money, I, like a fool, put it in a joint bank account with my husband. When we divorced, he got half."

- H.N., Charleston, SC

PUBLISHER'S PREFACE

Presenting over 100 seminars per year and having conducted thousands of personal estate planning sessions with the seminar attendees who ask to meet with him, Dan Recer probably has more direct experience in client contact than any estate planning professional in America.

Applying the wit, humor and clarity that have epitomized his seminars for over 20 years, Dr. Recer has written an engaging and useful book that shows how lay people can grasp the elements of estate planning. Using his system, they can design their own plan that will avoid the unhappy circumstances that surround so many family plans.

> "The last thing you want to leave
> your children is a fuss and a fight."

It is almost impossible to remedy the problems of poor estate planning. Families still pay far more taxes and create far more ill-will than can be undone.

Far better that families read and heed the simple solutions Dan so clearly presents in this wonderful, readable book.

Unlike most financially-oriented books, this one illustrates each concept with one of the multitude of stories Dan has gleaned from his thousands of personal estate planning sessions. Instead of quoting lengthy paragraphs from the IRS Rules and Regulations, Dan applies the truths of the Code using real-life, true stories that he lived when meeting with families in the 25 states where he has conducted seminars.

As a former college Vice President, a former technical sales executive and a former Presidential Appointee in the federal government, Dan Recer has a broad-based background. Calling upon all his experience in these roles, he has created a system that allows lay people to understand and to apply estate planning devices that save their hard-earned money and avoid years of family-rending misunderstanding and heartache.

Every Mother-in-Law in America will find helpful ideas in the pages of this book.

All Fathers-in-Law will find Dan's estate planning principles to be practical, understandable and valuable.

Whether you want to disinherit your Son-in-Law ... or to give him the key to the family vault ..., the Recer system will show you how to do it in the most cost-effective, private and expeditious way.

The modest investment of time and money required to read this book pales in comparison to the economic and emotional savings inherent in its pages.

In addition to serving as a text for lay people, this book will be a valuable resource for all financial professionals; it will show them how to translate the complexities of estate planning into terms their clients can easily understand and apply.

Dr. J. Dan Recer has plowed new ground by demystifying the complexities of estate planning and by translating the arcane professional Legalese into the everyday language of American business and society.

TABLE OF CONTENTS

LIST OF GRAPHICS

PROLOGUE

As a seminar speaker and estate planner, I conduct over 125 estate planning seminars each year. In addition, I have met with over 4,000 families in one-hour sessions who, after attending my seminars, asked for a personal estate planning session with me or with one of my staff members.

Unlike most professionals in the combined fields of financial and estate planning, I sell no financial product of any kind. I do not sell insurance, stocks or any other financial product. My services are paid for by the host, usually a non-profit organization or a bank trust department.

Repeat: I am not a stock or insurance hustler !

I have no license to sell stocks or insurance. So, if you are looking for a "Get-Rich-Quick" book on stocks or investments, you will have to go to another volume.

In Kingsport, Tennessee, where, for several years, I had the pleasure of working with the foundation executive, Bill Doyle, and with the late Jim Helton, a group of medical doctors sponsored my appearance and invited their members and spouses to attend.

At most of my seminars, the host organization provides a writing tablet for attendees to use for seminar notes. But at this particular seminar, through oversight, I suppose, no tablets were provided.

When I arrived at the part of the seminar where I show parents how to disinherit their sons-in-law ... and where I write the THREE SECRET WORDS OF ESTATE PLANNING on a flip chart .. there was considerable movement in the crowd as the audience searched their handbags and pockets for a pen and a writing surface.

Earnestly, each wrote down the THREE SECRET WORDS OF ESTATE PLANNING, words which are the key to disinheriting sons-in-law.

Reflecting on the seminar alone in my hotel room later in the evening, I realized the most important part of the seminar ... to the attendees ... had been the part where I showed them how to disinherit their in-laws.

In the seminar, I had covered about twenty estate planning concepts; but as far as the crowd was concerned that one part was most important.

With the passage of time, I continue to observe the seminar attendees' behavior and to note their words when they talk with me at the seminar break and when they come in for personal estate planning meetings. I observe that they are giving more and more attention to the in-law facet of estate planning.

On many occasions, personal estate planning counselees have said of their seminar attendance,

"I got that part about in-laws down in my notebook
and I am going to tell my attorney to include that in my plan."

Hence the first part of the title of this book:

"How to Disinherit Your Son-in-Law"

Another incident, this one in Easton, Maryland, is responsible for the second part of the title to this book. While designing a woman's personal estate plan two years ago, I was able to save her about $300,000 in federal estate taxes. When I finished her rather complex estate plan and showed her the $300,000 savings, she blurted out, *Does the IRS know about you?*

So the Easton woman gets credit for the second part of the book title,

"And Stiff the IRS"

The twin devils of disliked in-laws, on the one hand, and the fear and loathing for the IRS, on the other hand, are two common banes of many American's lives ... and of their estate plans.

You are busy with a thousand other facets of life and have had little opportunity to get informed on this subject. Hopefully, with the information contained in this book, you will be eminently qualified to design a super estate plan and to avoid the heartache of accidental disinheritance and the financial calamity of over-taxation.

After meeting with thousands of families in personal estate planning sessions, I know how frustrated people are with the present system and how much they want straightforward information with which to design their plans.

In this book I am going to explain the problems to you, detail some of the documents and strategies used in estate planning ... and show you how to design a plan that will disinherit your son-in-law ... and stiff the IRS.

If I am able to help you do either, I will be greatly gratified and will feel, as I do at the end of most of my seminars, that I have been able to make a significant intellectual contribution to my fellow human beings.

Oakton, Virginia
Spring, 1997

CHAPTER ONE

THE SMILING SON-IN-LAW

In-laws inherit many American estates.

Untold numbers of parents enrich their in-laws.

Via clumsy, errant or lazy estate planning, tremendous numbers of in-laws fall into significant inheritances.

When I mentioned this fact in to a group of medical center executives in early 1997, one of the women piped up and said,

"That's what happened to me."

She continued, "When my mother died and left me an inheritance, I, like an idiot, went down to the bank and put all the money into a joint bank account with my husband.

"Later," she resumed, "when we divorced, the court held that the money in the bank account was community property and that my ex-husband would get half of it."

Graphic 1.1 illustrates the smiling son-in-law scenario.

"Hopefully, you don't think that you are the only person who ever created an accidental disinheritance scenario for themselves," I sympathized. "I have met many people who did exactly what you did … and many who did things of a similar nature."

"Well, anybody in their right mind wouldn't do what I did," she replied. "They would know that putting names on a bank account jointly would enable the other spouse to get half of the money in the event of divorce."

I said, "If all the people who put their spouse's name jointly on a bank account were not "in their right mind", I am afraid we

GRAPHIC 1.1

THE SMILING SON-IN-LAW

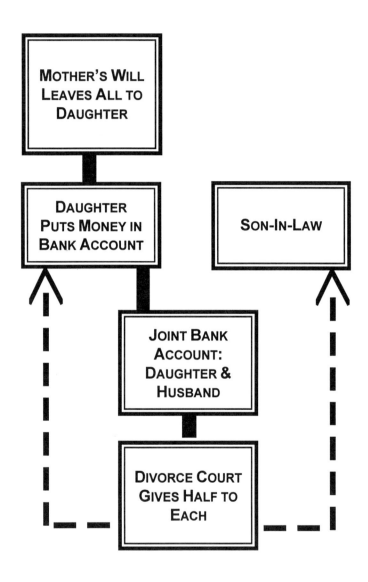

would have a majority of Americans who qualify for the mental ward."

In spite of all my well-intended apologies, she maintained that her actions demonstrated a moonstruck mentality.

She certainly was not a stupid person; she held a very responsible position in a major medical center. When she wound up with only half of her mother's inheritance, she mentally kicked herself and said, "I'm dimwitted for allowing this to happen to me."

The truth is that she handled the situation in a very typical manner.

No one likes to plan for the worst-case scenario; nobody wants to go into a marriage with a plan for withdrawal. But in today's social climate, it makes sense to be cautious.

What if, instead of leaving the money to her daughter "outright," this woman's mother had left the inheritance *in trust* for the daughter. Then, when the divorce transpired, the trust did not divorce the husband; the assets in the trust would have been safe.

Parents generally leave their entire estate to their children; in many cases they think that they are protecting their family's interest by "leaving it all to the kids."

They think they are keeping their assets in their blood line.

What these parents fail to consider is the probable second step in their children's handling of the inheritance.

The most typical second step in the progression is that the heir goes to the bank and deposits the money into a joint account with his/her spouse. Generally speaking, from that time forward, the money is no longer the property of one person. It has become joint property. In most divorce courts, joint property is divided between the parties.

Or the heir and spouse decide to use the money to purchase a new residence. When they take title to the new house, they usually take it with some form of joint ownership. Again, that joint property is deemed to be "theirs" by most divorce courts.

In a joint bank account, a joint stock account, or in some form of joint property ownership, the heir has co-mingled his/her assets with those of the spouse. In most such cases, divorce courts have held that the asset is a joint one. In community property states, the asset may have lost its one-spouse identity and may have become community property.

By mixing assets with the spouse, the heir has extinguished the paper trail that would have shown that the asset belonged to the one who inherited it.

Many states have laws that purport to keep the inheritance out of the estate of the heir's spouse ... and knowing this, families often depend on these state laws to protect their inheritance. They expect that these laws will keep their money in their blood line.

These laws are, generally, only operable if the inheritance is kept completely and distinctly separate from joint or marital ownership.

If, after inheriting the funds or securities ... and depositing them into a joint bank or stock account, the heir dies, the heir's spouse, the in-law, owns the account outright. The inheritance is now completely out of the family; out of the blood line. It has been completely transferred into another blood line; into another family's ownership.

In a bad-case scenario, the in-law re-marries, puts all the assets into joint accounts with the new spouse ... and dies.

The new spouse owns everything and, most likely, makes his/her children the beneficiaries of the estate.

Now the grandchildren of the original family progenitors, the couple who worked to earn the money in the first place, are totally disinherited. The assets have gone to strangers and the progenitors' (other) children and grandchildren are accidentally and completely disinherited.

Because we meet with hundreds of families in personal estate planning sessions each year, my staff and I hear many very interesting stories.

Following are some stories told to us by people who have come to us for their estate plans. In different ways, each story tells how in-laws affect estate planning and family wealth.

HOW AN EX-SON-IN-LAW ACQUIRED HIS WIFE'S INHERITANCE

A 1993 experience in Annapolis, Maryland, is the genesis for this story. The parents came in for an estate planning session and told me the story of their daughter and son-in-law.

While the daughter was single, the parents had given her one of their rental houses. When she married, she and her husband moved into it for their family residence and lived there for some time. After several years, they decided to sell that house and buy another.

The daughter, literally, sold the house because her name was on the deed as the sole owner.

However, when they bought the new house, they took title in the way that many married people do, "Joint Tenants With Right of Survivorship", (JTROS). This means they are joint owners, and if one dies, the survivor of them is the owner.

Some years later, and after producing three children, the couple divorced.

Among other orders, the divorce decree awarded the son-in-law the right to sell the house and to keep one half of the proceeds.

On learning of the court's decision, the daughter's family was, of course, shocked and angry. As far as they were concerned, the house they had given to their daughter was intended to belong to her and, they reasoned, any house purchased with the proceeds of the sale of the gifted house should also belong only to their daughter.

By taking title to the second house jointly with her husband, the daughter had legally forfeited her sole ownership of the property ... and of the "inheritance" her parents had wanted to give her during their lives.

Graphic 1.2 illustrates the grinning son-in-law scenario.

Half of the money they provided their daughter flew out the window ... and into the eager hands of their son-in-law.

Contrary to the parents' reasoning, the judge ruled that the joint property was divisible in the divorce even though it was purchased with assets given from the wife's family.

5

GRAPHIC 1.2

THE GRINNING SON-IN-LAW

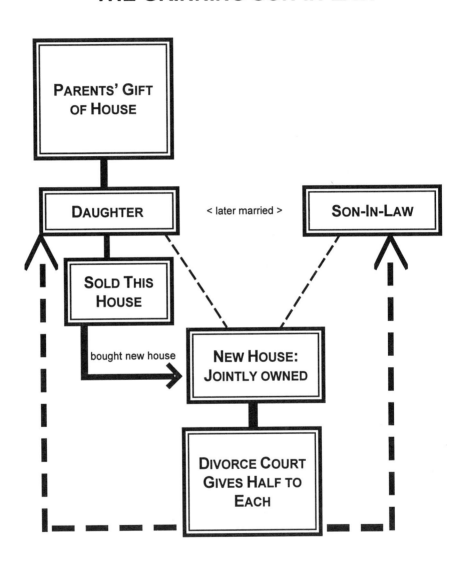

It is easy to see how gifted property or inherited property can become marital property for purposes of divorce. This case is more like what really happens. People do sell houses, move to other houses and take title as they please.

Do not ever count on the inheritance laws of your state to protect your child from divorce court. The newspapers are full of strange and amazing stories of divorce settlements that often appear to be grossly unfair.

I cannot finish this story without telling the epilogue.

The ex-son-in-law has married twice since that original divorce; has divorced both successive wives and received similar settlements in each case. According to the couple with whom I met, he is now awaiting the death of an 83-year-old mother-in-law before divorcing his current wife.

Evidently, he has learned the system well ... and is using his knowledge to increase his net worth and to build his estate.

THE PRIME CORNER OF LAND: NOW OWNED BY STRANGERS

In the Shenandoah Valley, a physician and his wife scheduled a late evening appointment for their estate planning session. They were about 15 minutes overdue when they arrived.

"I had to go feed the cows after we closed the practice," the doctor apologized.

Then he proceeded to tell me their family situation.

Twenty years earlier, he and his wife had found what to them was a diamond in the rough ... a run-down farm centered around a dilapidated classic Greek revival home ... and situated in the verdant Shenandoah Valley at the foot of the massive Massanutten mountain.

Both had dreamed of such a place as their eventual, family home ... and each enjoyed the anticipated hands-on work of restoring the buildings and grounds to their former grandeur.

Purchasing the farm, they set about to restore house, barns, outbuildings and fences so they would have a beautiful place to live

7

and so the doctor could realize his dream of owning a herd of prize cattle.

As the years went on and their daughters joined in the restoration work, the family's combined efforts began to change the appearance of the entire place. After many years of diligent labor, the farm blossomed into the beautiful home they had envisioned.

After college, one of the daughters announced her intention to marry and expressed interest in staying right in the area.

Wanting her to continue to enjoy the beauty of the Shenandoah, the fruits of the family's combined labor and the view of the mountain, the physician and his wife decided to deed the best corner of the land to her and her bridegroom as a wedding present.

Delighted with the present, the young couple built a house on the prized crown corner of the farm.

But alas, after a few years, the young couple divorced.

When the domestic affairs judge ordered the house sold and the proceeds divided, the doctor and his wife had no funds with which to re-purchase the corner. All their extra money was invested in the farm's redevelopment and in the doctor's practice.

Strangers purchased the house for their residence.

"Now," the doctor explained, "I drive past the house on the beautiful corner of our land each time I go and come from my office. It breaks my heart that strangers now own the best corner of our farm that we worked so long to pay for and to restore."

With perfectly good intentions, the doctor/farmer and his wife had forfeited one of the most precious pieces of their beloved estate.

Now, instead of its belonging to them and to the daughters who assisted in the restoration, strangers enjoy the fruits of the family's labor.

"THEY TOOK EVERYTHING BEFORE I RETURNED FROM THE FUNERAL"

In Pittsburgh, an elderly man stood up in the seminar and said to me and to the crowd, "Let me tell you my story."

I gave him the floor.

He related that he and his second wife had married later in life and that he had agreed to sell his home and all his household goods and to move into her home.

Both had children by previous marriages.

After some years, she died.

"When I returned from the funeral, her kids had scavenged the house. They had taken almost every stick of furniture and all her other belongings," he reported. "To have enough furniture to live comfortably, I had to go out and buy everything I needed."

The man didn't claim to know how people could protect themselves from such circumstances; but he warned the entire audience about the folly of poor planning.

Later that night, alone in my hotel room, I thought about the elderly gentleman's story.

Probably the lady's children had no legal basis on which to come and claim her possessions. Often adult children have their eyes on certain things, and sometimes, in their minds, they own it, "... when Mother dies."

Could he have taken legal action against them and prosecuted for grand theft?

Perhaps. But what would it have gained him?

No doubt he would have spent more time and effort than he would have gained.

THE MEAT OUT OF THE FREEZER!

A woman on Maryland's Eastern Shore told a similar story about the death of her second husband.

Explaining how her late husband's children had, after his death, demanded half of all their joint possessions, she described how they came to her home and took half of everything that the couple had owned.

She exclaimed, "They even took half the meat out of the freezer."

CAN YOU PLAN YOUR ESTATE TO PREVENT SUCH ABUSE?

What is it in the character of human beings that turns apparently reasonable people into snarling scratching scavengers at the death of a family member?

Why do people demonstrate such dramatic change when a family member dies?

Did they actually change?

Or were they for years, masking their greedy grasping acquisitive nature?

Not being a psychologist, I don't know the answer.

I do know that many people behave far differently toward their siblings and in-laws after the death of a family member than before. Old animosities fester into feverish sores of malice, suspicion and revulsion.

Perhaps a mother's death removes the glue that held the family together. Feeling no continued governor for their ancient revulsion, jealousies surface and create gigantic fissures between people who, at one time, related amicably.

Maybe she was their only common bond. Perhaps many family members have been holding their sibling anger to themselves in an effort to shield Mother from psychic pain, ... and when Mother dies, they no longer feel restrained from venting their pent-up malice.

While I cannot identify the root cause of the change that often occurs, I can help you prepare for any possible change. I cannot prevent the familial ruptures; but I can show you how to keep those family fissures from causing you economic hardship.

The good news is that you can arrange your affairs so that you control the entire scene. You can protect your heirs from the changes that actually or apparently transpire in people's hearts after you are gone.

Good estate plans are created only when people are willing to listen, read, learn and persevere through good and bad advice, narrow-minded advisors and a system that is stacked against effective planning.

10

Be like the physician in Baltimore who came to me with a three-inch stack of documents and said, "I think my attorney did what I wanted; but I want you to read the documents to be sure.

"I would be so relieved if you would read all these documents and tell me exactly what they mean. I don't want to sign them until I know that this is the plan that I had in my head when I went to the attorney."

Read, listen and learn. Then outline and implement. As in most areas of life, there is no one who will look out for your interests as well as you can. Yes, it may be hard work. You may meet with many frustrations along the way.

But the peace of mind you gain from the process will be well worth the effort. You have worked a lifetime to gain your material, social and familial riches. Certainly a few hours of diligent work is not too much of a sacrifice to ensure that your estate planning desires become reality.

FUN QUIZ

ON THE MATERIAL IN CHAPTER ONE

1. T F When children divorce, the judge always returns gifted property back to the parents who gave it.

2. T F Joint ownership with right of survivorship means "if one dies, the other owns the property."

3. T F Money in a joint bank account belongs to the survivor.

4. T F A family member's death usually brings out the best in the family and the in-laws.

5. T F Stock can be held in a joint account.

Test answers are shown on Page 213.

CHAPTER TWO

HE WANTED HIS FATHER-IN-LAW . . . DEAD

During a day of conducting personal estate planning sessions in a small town on the Chesapeake Bay, I met with a woman whom I will call Nan Hill. She told me, "My husband, Bob, and I have worked all our lives to get what we have. We started out renting one small farm. After several years we were able to buy it ... and over the years and with much hard work, we have acquired additional land."

She concluded, "We now have four farms."

"How can I help you?" I inquired.

She said, "When I heard you speak at the seminar, I thought you might be able to help us solve our problem. I came to see you because Bob and I are very concerned with keeping our possessions for our own family.

"We have four daughters, all married. So, we also have four sons-in-law."

Then, as if the very words pained her body and soul, she said, "We get along fine with all of these daughters and these sons-in-law ... except for one son-in-law ... and we don't like him very well."

She paused, finally adding, "In fact, we despise him."

"Why is that?" I asked.

"When my husband got hurt on the tractor and was hospitalized with his injuries, we know that this son-in-law went to a neighbor's house and told them that he wished Bob would go ahead and die ... so he would get his farm.

"Dr. Recer, can you tell me how to be sure he *never* gets one of our farms?"

"Of course I can," I replied in a voice I hoped would conceal my shock.

"As you surmised from attending the seminar, I talk with a wide variety of people who bring a multitude of family and financial problems to the table. While you are the first one to tell me that an in-law actually wanted someone to die, you are not the first to express a desire to keep the family's assets out of the reach of in-laws.

"My associates and I have designed estate plans for scores of people who express similar desires."

I encouraged her to relax and to give me a full understanding of the whole situation. "First, tell me a little more about your family and about the farms so I can grasp the entire picture."

She said each of her daughters had two children and that the farms, in toto, were worth about $2 million.

"Bob and I paid only about $50,000 for the farms," she said. "Of course, that was over a long period of years. When the highway came through, the price of land increased and several farms have sold for many times their original value."

" I suppose that the two of you own the farms jointly?" I asked her.

"Yes, both of our names are on the deeds. Here, I can show them to you," she said, pulling some papers out of her purse.

Reviewing the deeds, I could see the couple owned the farms jointly. They owned "Joint Tenants With Right of Survivorship." This form of ownership is abbreviated JTWROS, or more often, "JTROS."

Presently the family consisted of these generations:
Generation One, Bob and Nan. (GEN I)
Generation Two, the four daughters. (GEN II)
Generation Three, the eight grandchildren. (GEN III)

Having this information, I could see they needed a plan that would optimally benefit these three generations. The primary beneficiaries would be Nan and Bob, the farm owners.

After also providing benefits for the other two living generations, we would want to design a plan that *might* provide benefits to two or three unborn generations. At this point, it would be impossible to tell exactly how many total generations might benefit.

In most situations like this, we can assume that we will also directly benefit:

Generation Four, the great-grandchildren. (GEN IV)
Generation Five, the great-great-grandchildren. (GEN V)
Generation Six, the great-great-great grandchildren. (GEN VI)

Generally, in conditions like this, we use a Safety Net Trust (SNT), a trust that holds the assets for the benefit of one or more of the family generations. Properly drawn, a SNT might stay in effect long enough to keep the family's assets out of the hands of in-laws, outside creditors and other strangers ... and to provide benefits to the family for about one hundred years.

While most people never think of keeping assets intact for that long, it is indeed possible to hold assets exclusively for the benefit of family members ... and out of the hands of in-laws ... for scores of years.

Almost immediately, I envisioned the plan.

I said, "In addition to disinheriting the son-in-law, I would expect that you would also want to avoid probate and taxes."

"Of course," she said emphatically.

I added, "Many of the people I deal with also want to exclude *other* in-laws from owning their assets."

"He's the only one we have had trouble with so far; but you are right. We do want *only* our own family to receive our assets."

I immediately proceeded to draw up the estate plan I would prescribe for her and her family. In brief, it included these documents and strategies; I listed them so she could see where we were going:

1. Two Living Revocable Trusts
2. Two Pour-Over Wills
3. Two Springing Limited Attorney Powers
4. Two Medical Powers of Attorney
5. Two Living Wills
6. Authorization, within the Living Trusts, for Bypass Trusts

7. Authorization, within the Living Trusts, for QTIP Trusts
8. A Safety-Net Trust
9. A Crummey Trust
10. Orders for the Bypass and QTIP to pour into the Safety Net at the death of the last of GEN I
11. The Three Secret Words of Estate Planning
12. The Two Back-Up Words of Estate Planning
13. The Family Limited Partnership
14. Shrinking the Estate
15. Generation Skipping

She was a bit nonplused when I listed all those estate planning elements.

"I thought we might just need a new will; ... that a simple plan would work for us."

"No one likes simplicity more than I do," I said. "Certainly we will keep the plan as simple as possible. But "simple wills" are often the cause of in-law inheritance ... and of a number of other very serious estate planning mistakes.

"Especially when parents, like you and Bob, own a farm or a business, the "simple will" approach can be a disaster."

I assured her I would explain each and every document and strategy carefully so she would understand all of my proposals so she and Bob could intelligently consider them.

"After we finish this meeting and after you and Bob take time to discuss my recommendations, I will be happy to meet with you again to review everything and to respond to any questions that may come up in your conversations."

To implement the plan, I explained that several carefully sequenced steps would be necessary. I emphasized that a comprehensive and efficacious plan would not be created overnight. It would not "just happen."

I could see that she was a gamer. A resolute woman, she had not come to dally. Instead, she had come to learn the game and to master it. She had not made the decision to seek my help lightly; and

I perceived that she would follow through and bring the plan to fruition.

She was determined to understand and to implement an estate plan that would create the greatest benefit for her family ... and that would allow both her and her husband to have the peace of mind they needed.

I assured her that, at the end of the game, they could be certain they were *not* allowing any of their assets to wind up in the hands of the son-in-law who had wished her husband dead.

I started demonstrating the requisite step-by-step process. For purposes of complete explanation, demonstrated in the next chapters are the steps that she and her husband would need to take ... and the resultant steps that would be implemented by a trustee after their deaths.

FUN QUIZ

CHAPTERS ONE THROUGH TWO

1. T F   It is impossible to disinherit an in-law.

2. T F   A good estate plan can benefit more than one generation.

3. T F   A Safety Net Trust is used only by circus performers.

4. T F   Probate can be avoided.

5. T F   A trust might eventually benefit unborn heirs.

Test answers are shown on Page 214.

CHAPTER THREE

WIPING THE SMILE OFF THE SON-IN-LAW'S FACE

Holding Nan Hill's story clearly in mind, knowing that her primary goal was to disinherit the son-in-law and having identified the elements that should comprise her estate plan, I was now ready to sequence the plan and to explain it to her in detail.

"This explanation will take some time," I warned. "Are you ready for a rather extensive recitation of details?"

She nodded and settling in her chair, prepared to take notes.

"We are going to approach this step-by-step," I assured her. "If at any time you feel you do not understand a specific step, just stop me ... and we will review it so you will easily comprehend. I am going to try to explain everything clearly so you will readily be able to relate the plan to your husband."

STEP NUMBER ONE: Clearly outline the family interrelationships.

While those who practice the purely financial approach to estate planning need no explanation of the family and its relationships, our approach requires a clear understanding of exactly how many family members there are ... and how each of them relate to the planners and to each other.

The first step we always take is to completely understand ... and to explain to the counselee ... exactly how many people will be... or can be ... impacted by the plan.

To do this, we usually use a full sheet of paper on which to outline the generations. Graphic 3.1 shows that there will definitely be *three* generations directly impacted. These are Gen I, Gen II and

THE HILL FAMILY GENERATIONS

**These Generations
Will Benefit**

**These Generations
May Benefit**

GEN I
NAN & BOB

GEN IV
GREAT-GRANDCHILDREN

GEN II
THEIR CHILDREN

GEN V
GREAT GREAT GRANDCHILDREN

GEN III
GRANDCHILDREN

GEN VI
GREAT GREAT GREAT GRANDCHILDREN

Gen III which represent the parents, their children and their grandchildren.

In addition to these three, it is possible that other generations *may* be impacted. It is highly likely that a family like this one could provide trust benefits for Gen IV, the unborn great-grandchildren. Benefits to Gen V and Gen VI, while increasingly less likely, are still within the realm of reason.

In Graphic 3.1 you can see that three generations *will* receive benefits and that three additional generations *may* become beneficiaries.

STEP NUMBER TWO: Create two living revocable trusts.

Each parent, Nan and Bob, would have a living revocable trust in order to protect assets from the probate process. Each of them would be his/her own:

> Trustor - creates the trust
> Trustee - manages the trust
> Beneficiary - as named by the trustor

Each would have the bank or stockbrokerage trust department as the Standby or Backup Trustee.

In addition, we would need a Standby Beneficiary of the LRTs. The Standby beneficiary of each of the two LRTs can be a person, a trust or a charitable organization. In this case, we will use a trust, a Safety Net Trust (SNT) that I will explain later.

All these LRT offices are shown in Graphic 3.2 where I have actually drawn a "picture" of two Living Revocable Trusts. On the left side of the boxes I have shown the office, ... on the right side, the person who fills the office. In Nan's LRT, for example, the office of trustee is filled by the incumbent, Nan.

Most likely you have never seen a picture of a trust. You have been led to believe that a trust is a mammoth mysterious configuration of words, phrases and polysyllables that can be understood only by lawyers.

Well, that isn't true. Graphic 3.2 is a picture of two trusts and it is certainly easy to understand.

GRAPHIC 3.2

NAN & BOB'S LIVING REVOCABLE TRUSTS (LRT)

NAN'S LRT

Trustor	Nan
Trustee	Nan
Standby Trustee	Bank
Beneficiary	Nan
Standby Beneficiary	SNT

BOB'S LRT

Trustor	Bob
Trustee	Bob
Standby Trustee	Bank
Beneficiary	Bob
Standby Beneficiary	SNT

STEP NUMBER THREE: Transfer the farms into the living revocable trusts.

In order to optimally utilize an LRT, we want to be sure that it actually owns something. We want to transfer assets into it during life.

When transferring real estate into LRTs, we actually change the deed so that each of the trustees of the living trusts become the new owners.

Bob, trustee of his LRT, will own half of the farms.

Nan, trustee of her LRT, will own half.

In my further explanations of this form of ownership, I will refer to "Bob T (Trustee) His LRT" and to "Nan T (Trustee) Her LRT."

No longer will they own each farm jointly (JTROS); they will each own half of each farm in their trustee roles. The form of ownership will be "Tenants in Common (TIC)."

By changing from JTROS to a TIC form of ownership, we employ an excellent estate planning device; we split the estate. Later, I will show you that this strategy will save taxes.

Graphic 3.3 illustrates the transfer of assets into the two Living Revocable Trusts.

STEP NUMBER FOUR: Create the other documents that, along with the Living Revocable Trust, constitute a Basic Estate Plan.

A Basic Estate Plan, for many people, consists of:

1. A Living Revocable Trust
2. A Pour-Over Will
3. A Business Power of Attorney
4. A Medical Power of Attorney
5. A Living Will

Most of the families with which we deal in our estate planning practice need all of the above-listed documents.

To ascertain that any assets not transferred to the living revocable trust during the trustor's life would go into the LRT at death, we use the Pour-Over Will.

TRANSFER ASSETS TO LRTs

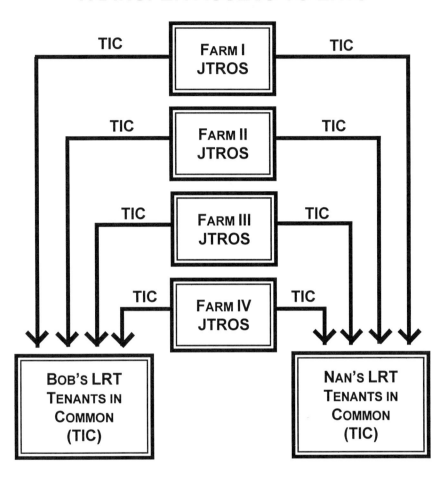

THE NEW OWNERS ARE:
BOB T (TRUSTEE) - HIS LRT
AND
NAN T (TRUSTEE) - HER LRT

If, for example, Aunt Matilda died and left our couple a million dollars the day before one of them died, the dying spouse's part of the legacy would pass from the will, the Pour-Over Will, into the living revocable trust. Those assets would, of course, go through probate on their way from the will to the LRT.

The Pour-Over Will is a simple instrument that says, "I have a Living Revocable Trust and if I own anything outside the trust when I die, use this Pour-Over Will to 'pour' assets into the LRT."

Because everybody needs a Business Power of Attorney (BPOA) and a Medical Power of Attorney (MPOA), we would also create these documents.

The Business Power of Attorney gives someone the power to sign legal documents for any assets that are owned outside the living revocable trust. If we state that the Business Power of Attorney "springs" into existence if and when "two board-certified physicians determine that the person is incapable of running his/her business affairs," it is called a "springing" power of attorney.

We do not need a Business Power of Attorney for assets already transferred into the living revocable trust because we have named a Standby Trustee who would, at the person's incapacity, care for things inside the trust. The Business Power of Attorney person or institution serves the same function for things outside the trust as does the Standby Trustee for things inside the trust.

By having both a Business Power of Attorney and a Standby Trustee, we can be assured all our assets will be properly cared for in the case of our disability.

We need a Medical Power of Attorney to give someone power over our *body* if and when we needed medical attention and were unable to instruct the family or physician as to our wishes. The Business Power of Attorney gives someone power over our business. The Medical Power of Attorney, on the other hand, gives someone power over our body.

In many states the Medical Power of Attorney is one document with the Living Will. The two functions are merged into one document. In other jurisdictions the two functions are served by separate documents.

The Living Will says, in essence, "If I am being kept alive by a machine, I don't want to live that way."

The Medical Power of Attorney names a person to make medical decisions.

Therefore, in addition to Living Revocable Trusts (LRTs), Nan and Bob will need all of these documents. In our estate planning experience, most families need all of these documents; so we have designated this group of documents as a Basic Estate Plan.

As shown in Graphic 3.4 and 3.5, both Nan and Bob will need five documents in order to create their Basic Estate Plan.

STEP NUMBER FIVE: Create a family limited partnership.

In order to pass the farms to the family, the couple needed a family limited partnership. As a planning device, the family limited partnership has many extremely valuable traits. One of them is the fact that it has both "voting" and "non-voting" parties.

In this case we are interested in keeping the voting power, the *general* partnership interests, in the hands of the parents while, simultaneously, beginning a process of transferring non-voting, or *limited* partner, interests down the line for the benefit of heirs.

By moving the limited partner shares out of the parents' taxable estate, we can, in the long run, save federal estate tax. Often this approach can also save state estate or inheritance tax.

First, Nan and Bob, in their roles as trustees of their living revocable trusts (LRTs), would be both the general partners and the limited partners. To emphasize, one general partner of the partnership would be "Bob T His LRT."

"Nan T Her LRT" would be the other general partner.

In those roles, they would each also be limited partners.

As general partners, they would have all the authority to act for the partnership. As limited partners, they would have non-voting ownership rights.

He, trustee of his living revocable trust, would own one percent general partner interest. She, trustee of her living revocable trust, would own one percent general partner interest. Each of them,

GRAPHIC 3.4

BOB'S BASIC ESTATE PLAN

LIVING REVOCABLE TRUST
(LRT)

POUR-OVER WILL

BUSINESS
POWER OF ATTORNEY

MEDICAL
POWER OF ATTORNEY

LIVING WILL

27

GRAPHIC 3.5

NAN'S BASIC ESTATE PLAN

> LIVING REVOCABLE TRUST
> (LRT)

> POUR-OVER WILL

> BUSINESS
> POWER OF ATTORNEY

> MEDICAL
> POWER OF ATTORNEY

> LIVING WILL

as trustees of their living revocable trusts, would then own 49 percent as limited partners.

Each of the parents, Nan and Bob, would initially control 50 percent of the family limited partnership; one percent as general partner and forty-nine percent as limited partner.

Graphic 3.6 illustrates the composition of the Family Limited Partnership.

STEP NUMBER SIX: Create a Safety Net Trust (SNT).

As indicated in STEP NUMBER TWO, we will create an SNT.

To create a "vessel" or "bowl" into which the farm assets would be placed for the benefit of the family, we will need an SNT. This is an irrevocable, a not-revocable, trust that they, as creators of the trust, can design exactly as they want.

The SNT is a separate trust from the two LRTs.

Now we will have a total of three trusts. All will be living trusts because they become effective while the parents live. Two of them will be living revocable trusts (LRTs) and one will be a living not-revocable, or irrevocable, trust.

As stated in STEP NUMBER TWO, the SNT will be the Standby Beneficiary of the two LRTs.

In order to protect assets for the beneficiaries, we often recommend an SNT. When assets are transferred to it, they are literally owned by the Trustee for benefit of (FBO) the beneficiaries. We can then tell the Trustee exactly how we want him to benefit the heirs.

After almost twenty years of taking questions in seminars and in personal estate planning sessions, I am convinced that most families are better off with an SNT than with a plan that gives the money to the heirs outright.

As our society becomes more and more complex, we find that fewer and fewer people are capable of handling a substantial bonanza of inheritance. Therefore it is far better to benefit heirs through a trust than to give them money outright.

Best of all, we can keep assets out of the hands of in-laws and other predators by using an SNT.

THE FAMILY LIMITED PARTNERSHIP

ONE PERCENT G.P.	ONE PERCENT G.P.
BOB, T HIS LRT	NAN, T HER LRT

49 PERCENT L.P.	49 PERCENT L.P.
BOB, T HIS LRT	NAN, T HER LRT

Legend:
 G. P. = General Partner Shares which control
 L. P. = Limited Partner Shares which own,
    but don't manage or control

The key words in the Safety Net Trust would be the three secret words of estate planning; those words are
"ONLY MY ISSUE"
Nan and Bob's SNT trust would state that "only our issue" can ever benefit from this trust. It would guarantee only people in the blood line extending from them could ever derive any benefit from the trust.

The three secret words of estate planning are the key to disinheriting sons-in-law, daughters-in-law and anyone else who might, contrary to the wishes of the progenitor, lay some claim to the estate.

Note that when using the three secret words of estate planning, we are, in no manner, insulting or discrediting the in-laws; our language will, in no way, give anyone legal grounds upon which to bring a lawsuit against our trust.

By the use of the three secret words, we guarantee that no one can legitimately say in a lawsuit, "My father-in-law insulted me by making derogatory statements about me in his trust; therefore, I deserve compensation."

Next we showed our counselee how to design the benefits that the Safety Net Trust would provide to Generation Two, the four daughters. Even though we are stating that GEN III, the grandchildren, will be the eventual beneficiaries, we are, in no way, failing to provide for GEN II.

Our plan will state that, during their lives, the four daughters would be the only beneficiaries of the trust, except for education benefits to the grandchildren. As long as they breathe a breath of air, the daughters would receive these benefits:

1. All the income from the Safety Net Trust.
2. Five Percent (split among whatever number is living at a given time) of the trust'sassets, if they wanted it.
3. Anything else for the daughters' health, education, maintenance and support (HEMS).

A careful look at these benefits shows that the daughters will receive ample care; they will not be denied anything they need.

Benefits to the grandchildren while any member of GEN II is alive, would be *limited to education benefits*. Grandchildren would receive only education benefits as long as any of the daughters are alive.

Nan liked this provision. She said, "Bob and I did not have the advantage of a formal education; but we certainly want to help any of our grandchildren get all the training they want."

We would design the Safety Net Trust with the provision that the trust would pay "room, board, books, tuition and reasonable transportation" for a two-year or four-year degree at any accredited college or university.

We could also insert words that would allow a descendent to attend a trade school or some other form of positive educational activity. Most of the grandparents with whom I have dealt have no desire to control the lives of their heirs; they merely want to be sure their money goes for worthwhile causes.

While they ordinarily think of education as being a formal four-year degree, they are not opposed to any form of legitimate learning.

Most people realize that different grandchildren may be endowed with different talents, interests and abilities; so they are satisfied to allow the trustee to pay for any reasonable educational activity.

Graphic 3.7 illustrates the Safety Net Trust.

STEP NUMBER SEVEN: Include a generation skipping plan in the Safety Net Trust.

To conserve assets for the family as long as possible, we would be using the generation skipping technique (GenSkip). This technique can keep a portion of the assets in the family for approximately twenty-five additional years per generation skipped ... without estate taxation.

In some families, the entire estate can be kept intact and not taxed for an additional twenty-five years per skipped generation. In other families, with larger assets, it is impossible to skip with the entire estate. Each parent could skip with $1 million in assets.

GRAPHIC 3.7

THE SAFETY NET TRUST

```
Trustors .................. Bob & Nan
Trustee ................... Bank
Income Beneficiary ......... Daughters
Principal Beneficiary ....... Grandchildren
```

FEATURES

1. "Only my issue" shall benefit.
2. As long as any of them live, daughters are the only beneficiaries.*
3. While benefitting, daughters enjoy three benefits:
   a.) All income
   b.) Five percent, if they want it
   c.) HEMS, if they need it

*At any time, other generations can receive educational benefits.

If this couple presently had any great-grandchildren, we would recommend a *double* generation skip; but the rules state that we must have a living member of the family for any generation to whom we are skipping and, in this case, the youngest family members are grandchildren (GEN III).

With the generation skip, the eventually named beneficiaries of the Safety Net Trust would be a *class* of people called "Nan and Bob's grandchildren." By making the beneficiary "a class of people," we guarantee that any additional people, in this case, grandchildren, that might be added to the "class" would benefit in the same manner as those already living.

The grandparents now have eight grandchildren. By naming the class, we will be providing benefits for any later-born grandchildren.

However, to re-emphasize, we must have at least one living member of the class in order to name that class as beneficiaries.

In other words, you cannot name "a class of people called my future great-great grandchildren" as beneficiaries of the trust.

Although we cannot name an unborn class as the beneficiary, we can provide benefits to the desired people for about twenty-two years past a "life in being" at the death of the last grandparent. In effect, we can name unborn heirs as beneficiaries.

Because the trust would eventually benefit the grandchildren, thus skipping one generation (the children), we would need to be mindful of Generation Skipping Transfer Tax (GSTT). The GSTT law allows each citizen to skip one or more generations with as much as $1 million without payment of GSTT tax.

Note that I did *not* say that skipping transfers would automatically avoid federal estate tax (FET). The rules are different for GSTT and for FET; so planners must be cognizant of both sets of rules and must plan accordingly.

Our plan will make every effort to avoid both taxes: the GSTT and the FET.

Graphic 3.8 illustrates generation skipping.

GRAPHIC 3.8

GENERATION SKIPPING

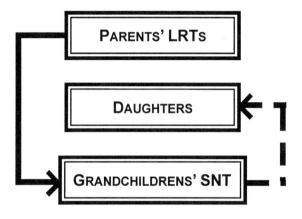

Legend:

━━━━━━━━ = **Principal**

▬ ▬ ▬ ▬ = **Income and Other Benefits**

In a $2 million estate, this approach could save over $300,000 in taxes.

STEP NUMBER EIGHT: Name a bank or stockbrokerage trust department as the trustee of the Safety Net Trust.

I explained to Nan the best trustee for the Safety Net Trust would be a bank or stockbrokerage trust department. Because of its professional expertise, objectivity and perpetuity, we think a trust department is the best trustee.

At first she thought this to be a strange suggestion. "Shouldn't my daughters be the trustee?" she asked.

While her reaction is a common one, most of our counselees eventually see that a corporate trustee is best.

After considerable explanation, Nan understood my reasoning that the family would need the stability, perpetuity, professionalism and objectivity of a corporate trustee.

Note that I did not recommend to her that an attorney or accountant be designated as trustee. While these professionals may be good people ... and some of them may understand all the jobs of a trustee, they can serve only in their *personal* role.

Their *firm* is not qualified, by state law, to serve as trustee ... and we don't want the family to be dependent on any single human being as trustee.

In other words, we want a corporation licensed to be a trustee in your state. Such corporations must demonstrate to your state officials that they are worthy of your trust. If more people would use these licensed corporations, you would read far fewer stories in the newspapers where ...

... "trustee steals money and flies to Rio."

There are other very good reasons for de-selecting personal professionals as the trustee, explained further in later chapters.

STEP NUMBER NINE: Design SNT benefits for other generations.

We then designed the benefits that would accrue to the grandchildren once all the daughters had died.

I suggested the trust state that, at the death of the last daughter, the grandchildren begin to receive the three benefits that had, up to their deaths, been accruing to the daughters.

Further, I suggested that the trust pay college cost for "any of our issue." With this provision, great-grandchildren and, possibly, two more generations (all unborn, of course) could receive their education cost from the trust.

STEP NUMBER TEN: Design the SNT's length.

Next, we decided upon the length of the trust. I suggested that she and her husband allow it to last as long as is legal. In effect, the legal length is about twenty-two years beyond the death of the last of her grandchildren.

With some very young grandchildren, and with the probability that some of them might live into their eighties or nineties, the trust might last a hundred years.

As each generation dies off, the next generation would step in and begin to receive benefits.

If Nan and Bob live another twenty years and, at their deaths, they have great-grandchildren, the trust could last even longer.

The trust can last the length of the longest living great-grandchild ... plus about twenty-two years.

The sum of those two numbers, the life span and the twenty-two years could easily total to a hundred. Perhaps even longer.

STEP NUMBER ELEVEN: Design the SNT to doubly protect the blood line.

To assure that no one ever "signs away" his benefits in the trust, we will use the two back-up words of estate planning:
"Not Assignable"
We will design the trust so that the benefits are *not* assignable. With this provision, no beneficiary can ever give away his benefits; he cannot sign away his beneficial interest in the trust. Not even if someone sticks a gun to his head and tells him to sign an "Assignment of Trust Benefits" document.

Under duress, a beneficiary might sign such a document; but our trustee will be under no obligation to honor the assignment. The trustee would always have the defense that the original makers of the trust, the trustors, had instructed him that trust benefits are "not assignable."

These back-up words also provide assurance that no divorce court could ever assign benefits from one of the beneficiaries to a divorcing ex-spouse.

STEP NUMBER TWELVE: In the LRT, authorize the Bypass Trust.

If Nan and Bob should die in a common accident, the assets in the two living revocable trusts would, for all practical purposes, pass directly into the Safety Net Trust. *Simultaneous* deaths would cause the Bypass Trust to *not* be fully utilized. To avoid the problem, the LRT document should say that despite the appearance of simultaneous deaths, one will be perceived to pre-decease the other.

But if the spouses die *sequentially*, as is usually the case, assets from the first spouse's estate would pass directly into a Bypass Trust which is designed to benefit the surviving spouse for his/her lifetime.

Each living revocable trust will say words like these, "If I am the first to die, I authorize my trustee to create a Bypass Trust, to fund it with the amount that is exempt from federal estate tax and to pay all the tax that will ever be due on the assets transferred to the Bypass Trust."

Thus the trustee would, under current law, transfer $600,000 into the Bypass Trust and would pay "all the tax that would ever be due," which would, of course, be zero.

We *want* to "pay the zero tax."

Why?

We are paying "all the tax that will ever be due." Once taxed, the Bypass Trust assets can *never* again be taxed.

The function of providing for a Bypass Trust allows a married couple to use two lifetime exemptions of $600,000. It allows them to pass $1,200,000 to heirs without payment of federal estate tax.

Normally, we want only a surviving spouse to be the life-income beneficiary of a Bypass Trust. He or she receives:

1. All income
2. Five percent of the trust corpus if spouse wants it

38

FUNDING THE BYPASS TRUST
AT BOB'S (FIRST) DEATH

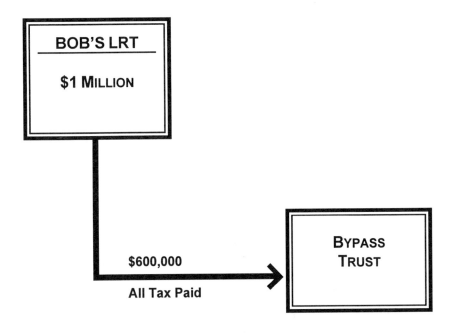

Nan retains her lifetime exemption of $600,000 and uses it at her death.

In summary, use of a Bypass Trust doubles the lifetime exemption for the couple. It becomes $1.2 million. This procedure saves $235,000 in tax.

3. Anything else for the spouse's health, education, maintenance and support (HEMS)

For the present, we will assume that each spouse has transferred $1 million to his/her Living Revocable Trust and that Bob then dies.

In Graphic 3.9, we assume that Bob is the first to die and we illustrate the passage to the Bypass Trust.

STEP NUMBER THIRTEEN: In the Living Revocable Trust, authorize the QTIP Trust.

When the first-to-die spouse has an estate exceeding the lifetime exemption amount, the estate plan also needs a QTIP trust, a Qualified Terminable Interest Property Trust, which also is designed to benefit the surviving spouse. Just as the first $600,000 is transferred to the Bypass, the remainder of the estate can be passed to the QTIP.

The living revocable trusts would authorize the trustee, at the death of the first spouse, to create the QTIP.

Any assets in the living revocable trust of the first-to-die spouse, over the $600,000 figure, would pass into the QTIP Trust where it would benefit the surviving spouse for his/her life.

During the life of the surviving spouse, all the benefits of the Bypass Trust and the QTIP Trust would accrue to that surviving spouse. These benefits would be the same ones noted for the daughters in the Safety Net Trust created in Step Number Two.

1. All income
2. Five percent of the trust corpus if spouse wants it
3. Anything else for the spouse's health, education, maintenance and support (HEMS)

During the life of the surviving spouse, no other heirs would ordinarily benefit from the Bypass and the QTIP. Under certain circumstances, the spouse could allow some income to be paid to children; but most families want these trusts to benefit only the surviving spouse during his/her life.

Assets in the QTIP are not taxed at the first death.

Why?

If assets over the $600,000 figure were taxed, the tax would not be zero. The next dollar would be taxed at thirty-seven percent.

However, the QTIP assets, no matter how large, are not taxed at the first death for the simple reason that these assets will benefit the spouse ... and the spousal rule of estate taxation says that the first spouse can leave *any* amount to the surviving spouse without taxation.

In Graphic 3.10, we again assume that Bob has $1 million when he dies; and we illustrate the passage of assets into the Bypass and into the QTIP.

STEP NUMBER FOURTEEN: At the death of second spouse, assets from the three trusts, Bypass and QTIP of first spouse and LRT of second spouse, pass into the Safety Net Trust.

Bypass trust assets would pass, without taxation, into the Safety Net Trust. There would be no deduction for taxes because we already "paid all the tax that would ever be due." One hundred percent of the Bypass Trust assets would pass directly into the Safety Net Trust.

All of the assets in the QTIP Trust, less any taxes owed, would pass into the Safety Net Trust.

The difference in the taxation of the Bypass and the QTIP lies in the fact that "all the tax that will ever be due" is paid on the Bypass when it is created.

The assets in the QTIP are, however, taxed when they pass from the benefit of the Gen I spouse to anyone else, in this case, when they pass to the Safety Net Trust.

In addition, all the assets, less taxes, belonging to the last-to-die spouse's Living Revocable Trust would pass directly into the family's Safety Net Trust.

So at the death of Gen I, Bob and Nan, the Safety Net Trust would be completely funded. Part of its funding might have come from gifts the couple made to it during life. Part of its funding would come from the second spouse's LRT. Part would come from the first spouse's Bypass and part would come from the first spouse's QTIP.

In sum, assets would find their way to the Safety Net Trust via four different avenues as shown in Graphic 3.11.

FUNDING THE QTIP TRUST
AT BOB'S (FIRST) DEATH

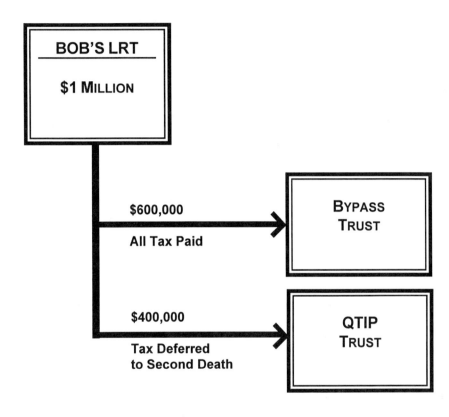

At Bob's death, IRS receives nothing.
On Bypass Trust, all tax is paid and it is zero.
On QTIP Trust, tax is deferred to Nan's death.

GRAPHIC 3.11

FUNDING THE SNT

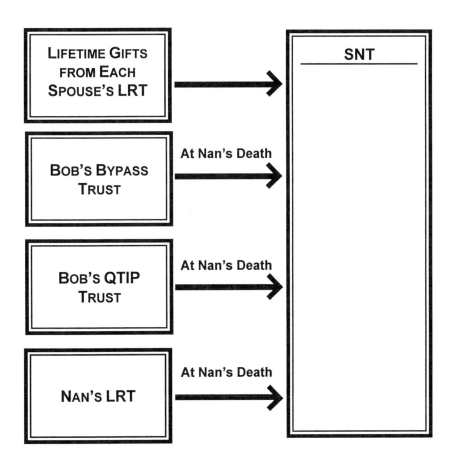

43

STEP NUMBER FIFTEEN: Make lifetime gifts to the SNT thus reducing the taxable estate.

By making gifts of limited partnership shares to the Safety Net Trust, we will reduce the value of the estate. We will reduce Bob and Nan's taxable estate.

We will move some limited partner shares into the SNT during Bob and Nan's life, thus reducing the number of shares in their at-death taxable estate.

Bob and Nan can use their annual exclusions from taxation to give as much as $10,000 worth of limited partner shares to each of the beneficiaries of the Safety Net Trust.

Or they can give $10,000 directly to the SNT, through the Crummey Trust, "for benefit of" each of the grandchildren. I will explain the Crummey Trust in a later paragraph.

If we count *only the grandchildren* as beneficiaries of the SNT trust, each of the grandchildren could give as much as $10,000 worth of limited partner shares to the Safety Net Trust for each of the grandchildren. Having eight grandchildren, each of the grandparents could move as much as $80,000 per year into the Safety Net Trust during their lives.

Together, the two grandparents could transfer as much as $160,000 to the SNT each year. They can make the "whether-or-not-to-give-this-year" decision each year. Creating the SNT does *not require* them to give every year.

There would be no gift or estate tax liability on these annual exclusion gifts. No tax when the gifts are made to the trust ... and no tax at Bob and Nan's deaths. Because these are annual exclusion gifts, they are excluded from gift tax.

Graphic 3.12 shows how we reduce the estate.

When reducing the taxable estate, we must contend with at least two kinds of transfer tax. We want to avoid both the Generation Skipping Transfer Tax and Federal Estate Tax.

As long as the total amount transferred (during life and death) from each grandparent is one million dollars or less, there will be no Generation Skipping Transfer Tax (GSTT).

GRAPHIC 3.12

REDUCING THE ESTATE

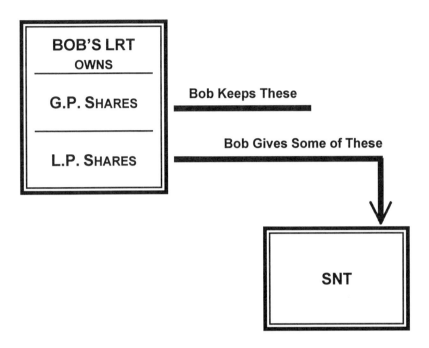

By giving away some limited partner shares, we reduce the parents' taxable estate.

In order to effect the movement of some limited partnership shares from the grandparents to the Safety Net Trust, we will use the Crummey Trust. Named for the man who conceived it, the Crummey Trust is an invaluable device used to make gifts and to decide how those gifts will be used. Actually, the shares will move rather rapidly *through the Crummey Trust* and into the Safety Net Trust.

STEP NUMBER SIXTEEN: Shrink the estate.

To further reduce the grandparents' estate, we will now employ a somewhat complex strategy known as "shrinking the estate." For taxation purposes, we will de-value each of the shares in the limited partnership.

Both kinds of shares, general and limited, will be taxation de-valued by about one-third.

Our justification for this shrinking lies in the fact that Bob and Nan will give only *limited* partner shares to the trusts. They will keep during their lives, the general partner shares.

Envision what would happen if the SNT trustee walked out onto Main Street, waved the limited partner shares in the air and said, "These are for sale. They are worth $10,000 per share. Who wants to buy them?"

A stranger walks up, examines the shares and declares, "They may be worth $10,000 to Bob because he is also the general partner; but if I bought them, I might not be able to sell them. They are not marketable."

Then the stranger pauses and says to the trustee, "I'll give you $7,000 per share."

The partnership has just shrunk by 30 percent.

Graphic 3.13 illustrates shrinking the estate.

For purposes of shrinking the estate, the total amount given in one year is a moot point. The amount is irrelevant. The mere fact that we give *any* amount combined with the fact that the recipient (trustee of the trust) can realize only a smaller market price for his shares is, in and of itself, enough evidence for us to shrink the estate.

Because a limited partner, which the trustee will be, has such little *control* over the partnership, IRS has agreed, in numerous cases, that

GRAPHIC 3.13

SHRINKING THE ESTATE

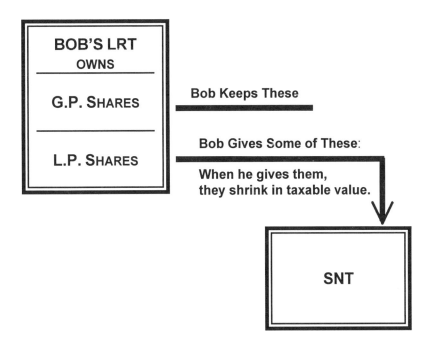

Because the SNT Trustee wil own only limited partner shares during Bob & Nan's lives, those shares are worth less than if he owned both limited and general shares. Hence, we shrink the taxable value of the estate.

the trustee's limited partnership shares are *worth less* than they would have been had all shares remained in the hands of the general partner.

Remember that we do *not* want the grandparents to give general partner shares to the SNT; they are to give *only* limited shares. By retaining all the general partner shares, the grandparents retain all control over the partnership during their lives. The general partnership shares will pass to the Safety Net Trust only when both Bob and Nan die.

One published list of about 25 estates that were thus shrunk produces an average decrease in market value of approximately 30 percent. It is safe to assume that we could shrink the value of the estate by nearly a third. Other planners have shrunk estates more than this amount; but we prefer to be conservative; so we will choose the 30 percent figure.

Because Bob and Nan's estate is valued at $2 million, we would apply the 30 percent shrinkage factor of $600,000 and come out with an estate valued, for taxation purposes, at about $1.4 million. We arrive at these figures by multiplying $2 million times 30 percent. This procedure gives us the $600,000 shrinkage figure. Then we subtract that $600,000 from the $2 million and arrive at the shrunken value of $1.4 million.

This shrinkage has immediately saved the family a tax, at the death of the last-to-die spouse, of about $250,000.

If this procedure seems to difficult for you to understand, read it again. It could be worth a quarter of a million dollars to your family. _____

Assuming that Bob and Nan choose to transfer $160,000 to the Safety Net Trust in the first and second year of the trust's creation, each GEN I spouse would then have, in his/her living revocable trust, general and limited partnership shares that have a total estate tax value of a little less than $600,000.

We get this figure by dividing their $1.4 million taxation value into two and finding that each would have about $700,000 in taxable assets. Then we reduce each of the estates by gifts of $160,000 and leave them with a taxable estate of $540,000 each.

If the two GEN I parents died the next day, after these transfers, there would be no federal estate tax because each of their taxable estates would be less than the $600,000 lifetime exemption amount.

The three means of tax avoidance of:

1. Reducing
2. Shrinking
3. Bypassing

... would have reduced each of their estates below the taxable point.

In this instance, we reduced the two grandparent's estates rather quickly. They could have chosen to give a much smaller amount to the Safety Net Trust during the early years and reduced the taxable estate more slowly. In any case, a judicious use of the annual exclusion gifts of $10,000 each can help the grandparents reduce their taxable estate to the $600,000 figure.

They could each transfer, over a period of years, enough limited partner shares to the Safety Net Trust to bring their (shrunken) taxable estate down to $600,000.

Done perfectly, this approach can allow the parents to pass their entire estate to the Safety Net Trust without payment of federal estate taxes.

In our experience of working with many farm and business families, we find that the more typical approach is to do *no* sophisticated planning and, at the last death to pay $588,000 in federal estate tax.

Although the approach that I showed Nan is somewhat complex, it saved nearly $600,000. That is worth learning some complexity, isn't it?

STEP NUMBER SEVENTEEN: Continue making $10,000 gifts to the Safety Net Trust.

Assuming some growth in the value of the estate as the years go by, the grandparents may need to make additional gifts of limited partnership shares to the Safety Net Trust to be sure that each of their (shrunken) estates is, at their deaths, no more than $600,000 in value. I suggested that they meet with their accountant in October of each year for a planning meeting. At that time they could assess their estate and, if it had grown during the year, could authorize their accountant to transfer additional limited partner shares to the Safety Net Trust.

STEP NUMBER EIGHTEEN: Benefits to daughters during parents' lives.

Remember that we are transferring only limited partner shares to the Safety Net Trust during the parents' lives. There will be very little "green money" in the trust. Only a portion of the net farm income proportionate to the number of limited partner shares owned by the trust would be paid to the trust each year. The daughters would realize a small income during the parents' lives.

There are several reasons this income will be very small.

The general partners will receive and disburse the income. Prior to disbursing the net income, they will pay all the real estate taxes on the farms and will pay all the operating costs of running the farm business.

One of those operating costs will be salaries for the managers. If Bob and Nan continue to actively manage the farms, they are entitled to reasonable salaries for their labors; a payment that comes out of gross income before net income is calculated.

Only the net income would be paid to the partners. Some of it would be paid to Bob and Nan, as general and limited partners. Some of it would be paid to the trustee of the Safety Net Trust, in his role as limited partner.

The trustee would pay the trust's expenses and would then disburse the remaining net income to the daughters.

Each year, the trustee will also file an income tax return for the trust. If the trust keeps no net income, this tax return will report the income received and the income paid out and will in effect say, "I had no net income; therefore, I owe no tax."

The bottom line is that there will be only a very small income paid to the daughters during the parents' lives. While that income will be taxable, the tax liability, like the income, will be very small.

50

Graphic 3.14 shows how the Family Limited Partnership works during Bob and Nan's lives.

Sensing that Nan had "had enough" of the planning process for a time, I suggested that we take a break and continue after we were mentally refreshed.

LIMITED PARTNERSHIP OPERATION DURING PARENTS' LIVES

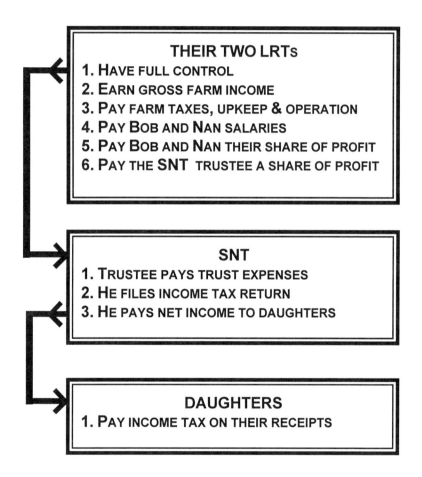

THEIR TWO LRTs
1. HAVE FULL CONTROL
2. EARN GROSS FARM INCOME
3. PAY FARM TAXES, UPKEEP & OPERATION
4. PAY BOB AND NAN SALARIES
5. PAY BOB AND NAN THEIR SHARE OF PROFIT
6. PAY THE SNT TRUSTEE A SHARE OF PROFIT

SNT
1. TRUSTEE PAYS TRUST EXPENSES
2. HE FILES INCOME TAX RETURN
3. HE PAYS NET INCOME TO DAUGHTERS

DAUGHTERS
1. PAY INCOME TAX ON THEIR RECEIPTS

FUN QUIZ

CHAPTERS ONE THROUGH THREE

1. T F GSTT refers to a great rock entertainment group.

2. T F A person can make a gift to a trust.

3. T F A Safety Net Trust can benefit children.

4. T F The annual exclusion from taxes can be used every year that the donor lives.

5. T F An important office of a trust is that of trustee.

6. T F The Bypass trust is used by single people.

7. T F The General Partner of a Partnership can be the Trustee of a Trust.

8. T F A QTIP provides income to the surviving spouse.

9. T F It would be smart to shrink an estate of $100,000.

10. T F The Living Revocable Trust is created at the death of the first-to-die spouse.

Test answers are shown on Page 215.

CHAPTER FOUR

TURNING HIS SMILE TO A GRIMACE

When Nan and I continued our discussion, I said, "Now, I am going to show you what will happen after you and your husband die. I am going to specify exactly what will happen to your estate after you and Bob are gone."

STEP NUMBER NINETEEN: At last to die of Bob and Nan, the trustee, acting "for benefit of" (FBO) the family, becomes the general partner.

Passing their remaining limited partner shares and their general partner shares to the Safety Net Trust through the Bypass Trust, the QTIP Trust and the Living Revocable Trust, the parents will, of course, relinquish their management responsibilities at the death of the last of them ... and will transfer those responsibilities to the Safety Net Trust Trustee.

(If Bob's estate was valued at $600,000 or less at his death, we would not have funded the QTIP Trust; hence, it would *not* exist and would *not* pour assets into the Safety Net Trust. QTIP Trusts are funded only with the over-$600,000 portion of the estate of the first-to-die spouse.)

The trust department, as Safety Net Trustee, will then own the assets in the trusts FBO the family.

If so authorized by the SNT trust document, the trustee will sell the farms, place all the proceeds into the SNT trust and begin paying benefits to the daughters. In effect, the trustee would replace the farms with cash and would pay the benefits to the heirs from those cash assets. At that moment, the trust would no longer own farms; it would own cash.

STEP NUMBER TWENTY: When one daughter dies.

We recommended that the parents make their daughters "lifetime beneficiaries with right of survivorship."

By using these words, the parents guarantee that the trust benefits stay in Generation Two as long as any of the daughters live. We like this approach because it provides for the one daughter who might live to be a hundred. There is no way we can tell how much money she might need by that time.

During the lives of any one (or more) of the daughters, the other generations receive only education benefits. When Bob and Nan design the trust, they can decide whether they want the grandchildren and successive generations to receive their education benefits from trust income, from trust principal or partially from both.

In our experience most grandparents choose to say,

"I want them to get an education, even if it takes
money from the trust principal."

STEP NUMBER TWENTY-ONE: At death of all daughters.

When all the daughters die, the three benefits of the trust accrue to Generation Three; Bob and Nan's grandchildren.

Generation Three, the grandchildren, receive:

1. All income
2. Five percent aggregated, if they want it; *not* five percent each.
3. Anything else, if they need it

Simultaneously, education benefits accrue to any and all other living generations. Great-grandchildren (Gen IV) could receive their education advantages while their (bloodline) parents are receiving the three above-named benefits of the trust.

If other generations (Gen V or Gen VI) were born before the twenty-two year rule had expired, they could also benefit from the Safety Net Trust.

STEP NUMBER TWENTY-TWO: The end of the Safety Net Trust.

As stated previously, the SNT trust can continue for about twenty-two years past the life of someone who is living at the death of the last of Bob and Nan. If at the last death of Bob and Nan, only grandchildren are living, the trust can continue for nearly twenty-two years past the life of the last of the grandchildren (Gen III).

If there are great-grandchildren at Bob or Nan's death, the trust could continue until nearly twenty-two years past the life of the great-grandchildren (Gen IV).

It is easy to see that the trust could, conceivably, continue for over a hundred years.

At the end of the trust, most families will divide the assets among the then-living heirs. Some families will also make provision for charity at that time.

At no time during the length of the entire estate plan would any son-in-law (or any other in-law) receive any direct benefits from the parents' estate.

If a daughter received her share of income from the trust principal ... and then took her husband out to dinner, a son-in-law would receive some indirect benefit. But it would be minor and it would not entitle him to any additional income benefit.

At no time would he ever be entitled to any portion of the trust principal, the main body of money.

All sons-in-law would be disinherited.

FUN QUIZ

CHAPTERS ONE THROUGH FOUR

1. T F   The GSTT exemption is $1 million.

2. T F   A trustee can legally do exactly as he pleases.

3. T F   Daughters can be "beneficiaries with right of survivorship."

4. T F   A person's annual exclusion can be used every year for 22 years after his death.

5. T F   At death of the farm couple, assets pass from the Safety Net Trust into the Bypass Trust.

6. T F   The Bypass trust can be used only by a married person.

7. T F   With 8 grandchildren, the farmer can use his lifetime exemption 8 times each year.

8. T F   A QTIP provides income directly to the IRS during the life of the surviving spouse.

9. T F   A trustee owns assets "for benefit of" others.

10. T F   The Living Revocable Trust saves probate fees.

Test answers are shown on Page 216.

CHAPTER FIVE

THE SON-IN-LAW'S DISINHERITANCE: A RECAP

By this time, Nan was mentally exhausted. But, to her credit, she had stuck with me through the entire process. Taking copious notes and asking for explanations and re-statements when needed, she had acquired a reasonable first-cut understanding of each of the estate plan elements.

Let's recap what we did for Bob and Nan.

1. We created and funded two Living Revocable Trusts to avoid the time, expense and heartache of probate.

2. We created two Pour-Over Wills to be sure that any "out-of-trust" assets would be poured into the trust at death. In this case, we were not forced to actually use the Pour-Over Will because the Living Revocable Trusts were completely funded during life. There *should* be no "out-of-trust" residue to be passed by the Pour-Over Wills; but we always want to have the Pour-Over Will included in the estate plan "just in case."

3. We created two Springing Limited Attorney Powers for use in the event that one of our principal people became incapacitated and needed someone to sign legal papers for them.

4. We created two Medical Powers of Attorney in case one partner needed medical care at a time when he/she was unable to make decisions.

5. We created two Living Wills that say, "If I am being kept alive by a machine, I don't want to live that way."

6. We authorized two Bypass Trusts and used one of those authorizations when Bob died. At Bob's death, we funded the Bypass

Trust with $600,000 worth of assets. The Bypass Trust then provided benefits to Nan for her life.

7. We authorized two QTIP Trusts and, if Bob's (shrunken) estate had been valued at more than $600,000 when he died, we would have implemented one of the authorized QTIP trusts. Then we would have funded it (with the over-$600,000 portion of his estate) and used it to benefit Nan for her life.

8. We created a Safety Net Trust and funded it partially during life and partially at the death of the last member of GEN I. During Bob and Nan's life, we made gifts to the SNT.

9. We used the Crummey Trust as a vehicle through which lifetime gift assets passed from the Living Revocable Trusts to the Safety Net Trust. Only lifetime gifts pass through the Crummey Trust. Legacies, on the other hand, do not utilize the Crummey Trust.

10. At Nan's death, we passed the Bypass Trust and her Living Revocable Trust into the SNT. If Bob's QTIP Trust had been funded, we would also have poured it into the SNT at this time.

11. To be sure that no outsider received any benefits from the Bob and Nan's estates, we used The Three Secret Words of Estate Planning, "only our issue."

12. To doubly insure that assets stay in the family, we used The Two Back-Up Words of Estate Planning, "not assignable."

13. To divide the farms into smaller "parts," we created a Family Limited Partnership, keeping the general (controlling) shares in the hands of the grandparents during their lives. Simultaneously, we transferred, by lifetime gifts, some limited partner shares through the Crummey Trust and into the Safety Net Trust for the benefit of the family.

14. To reduce the taxable value of the estate, we shrank it for purposes of estate taxation.

15. To avoid the repetitive taxation of the same asset, we skipped generations.

By designing all these steps and by creating the documents that would implement them, Bob and Nan could rest assured that their hard-earned estate would benefit only their intended loved ones.

"We have accomplished everything I wanted," she pronounced.

"While I had no idea it would take all those steps to achieve what Bob and I wanted to do, I feel good about the plan and I'm glad I was able to understand each step."

She shook my hand with a certain pride of accomplishment. As Nan walked away, she carried herself with confidence and aplomb. Her body language conveyed her new assurance.

It almost shouted out to the son-in-law,

"You're *not* going to get our money."

FUN QUIZ

CHAPTERS ONE THROUGH FIVE

1. T F The GSTT exemption and the FET exemption are identical amounts.

2. T F A trustee works FBO others.

3. T F Daughters can be beneficiaries for only 22 years.

4. T F Each partner in a marriage has an annual exclusion of $10,000.

5. T F When funding the Bypass Trust, we pay "all the tax that will ever be due" on any amount up to the lifetime exemption figure.

6. T F At death of the surviving spouse, both a Bypass and a QTIP Trust can be created.

7. T F With 8 grandchildren, the farmer can use his annual exclusion 8 times each year.

8. T F One can use the generation skip to skip as many as 22 generations.

9. T F The Safety Net Trust can be partially funded during life and partially funded at death.

10. T F The Pour-Over Will moves assets into the Living Revocable Trust at death of the Trustor.

Test answers are shown on Page 217.

CHAPTER SIX

MAKING SURE HE NEVER SMILES AGAIN

EXACTLY HOW TO DISINHERIT YOUR SON-IN-LAW:

Most planners intend for their own family to receive the benefits of any inheritance. While most of them harbor no animus for their in-laws, they generally want their own heirs to inherit.

Unfortunately, assets are often accidentally scattered like November leaves among direct descendants and in-laws. In many cases, the assets wind up outside the family because of a divorce or an untimely death in the next generation.

If you want your assets to benefit only your children, grandchildren and great-grandchildren, you may want to create a trust that protects their interest. As stated previously, we call this trust the Safety Net Trust (SNT).

You can create this trust and direct that it is to benefit "only my issue." By including this phrase and by directing the trustee to pay out only certain benefits to the heirs while retaining the corpus or body of money, you protect the estate.

By including this phrase ... and by paying close attention to the other details of the trust, you can create a trust that will never pay out any benefit to a son-in-law or daughter-in-law.

You can "Divorce Proof" your estate plan. You can guarantee that your assets will not be lost in a divorce of your children, grandchildren or great-grandchildren.

In the trust, you can then list the kinds of benefits that you want your heirs to receive. These might include health, education, disability protection, educational travel, etc. With prescriptions such as these, your trustee can use the money only for your approved purposes. He cannot use it for anything contrary to your intentions.

Once the Safety Net Trust is created, you can fund it by making lifetime gifts to it and/or making a final gift to it at your death.

Of course this final gift might be channeled through one or more of a number of vehicles. Some might come through your Living Revocable Trust. Some might pass from your ... or your spouse's ... Bypass Trust, etc.

HOW TO DIVORCE-PROOF YOUR DAUGHTER'S INHERITANCE

Recognizing that many families' estates are wholly or partially lost when an heir receives an inheritance ... and when the heir is subsequently divorced, many states now have laws that specify what assets are to remain in the marital estate. In other words, state lawmakers have tried to avoid estate loss through heirs' divorces.

For these laws, the legislatures are to be commended.

However, families should *not* depend on these laws to protect their heirs.

Why?

Because many heirs commingle their inherited assets with other assets; thus allowing the asset to lose its "inherited" character.

For example, you leave your married daughter $100,000 and she, subsequently, uses that money as a down payment on a home ... and she and her husband take title to the home jointly. That $100,000 has lost its inherited character because the house is a joint asset.

In such a case, the separate asset has been converted into a joint asset by the heir's taking title to the house "Joint Tenants With Right of Survivorship."

While each state's laws and court proceedings are different, one can readily see how inherited property can easily become joint property.

To avoid losing assets to an heir's subsequent divorce, you should consider using an irrevocable trust ... a not-revocable trust ... into which you can pour the assets. If you name a bank or stockbrokerage trust department as the trustee and if you state in that irrevocable trust exactly how you want assets to pass, you have divorce-proofed the inheritance.

A Safety-Net Trust is the best vehicle for protecting your heirs from losing your money in their divorce. You can set it up now and begin making gifts to it ... and at death make a final gift through your will or living revocable trust.

Or you can create, or authorize, the trust now and fund it entirely at your death from your will or from your living revocable trust.

DISINHERITING STEP-GRANDCHILDREN

Given today's social setting with so many blended families, it is sometimes difficult to wade through the way you want your estate to be distributed. Many families have children, step-children, grandchildren and step-grandchildren. In nearly every state, you can decide exactly how you want all these people to benefit.

A Baltimore couple came in for estate planning in the spring of 1993 and told me that they had an estate of $300,000 and that their family consisted of four children, all married. Two of their children had children of their own. Two had none of their own; but had step-children. The family consisted of three generations, Gen I, Gen II and Gen III.

The parents wanted only their own blood line to benefit from their estate. They wanted to provide nothing for step-grandchildren. They wanted the estate to go to their four children "with right of survivorship" prior to going to grandchildren.

In other words, they wanted *each* of their children to enjoy the benefit of the parents' estate. When one of their children died, they wanted the benefits to continue ... and to go to the three *remaining* children. At the death of a second child, the remaining two would benefit, etc. Eventually the one surviving child would become the sole beneficiary.

No benefits were to be provided for grandchildren until the last of their children died.

The only way to accomplish this goal is to use a trust. In this case, I recommended a Safety Net Trust (SNT).

To start with, the parents (Gen I) would place their assets into a Living Revocable Trust which would become, at the death of the last parent, a Safety Net Trust. At the death, it would become an irrevocable (not-revocable) SNT trust.

Instead of benefiting the children directly, we would conduct a generation skip and make the trust for the (eventual) benefit of the four grandchildren (Gen III) (excluding step-grandchildren).

During the children's lives, after the parents died, income would go to them (Gen II) with right of survivorship.

The grandchildren would *not* benefit until all the children had died. Meanwhile, when all four children (Gen II) were alive, all would receive income; one dies, three would receive income, etc.

Until the last of Generation II died, the grandchildren would receive nothing. In addition, no step-grandchild would benefit ... and no spouse in Gen II or Gen III would benefit.

Because the couple knew exactly what they wanted, it was rather easy to design their estate plan.

Our plan guaranteed that there would never be any "in-law" inheritance ... and there would never be any "step" inheritance.

SPOUSES' INHERITANCE RIGHTS

Spouses have special rights ... and should be given special consideration ... in estate planning.

Even though all states recognize a marriage created in other states, the word "marriage" doesn't mean exactly the same thing in each state. The word has different meanings when applied to a surviving spouse's rights.

Marriage and divorce laws are different in each state; therefore you cannot count on the law of your state being the same in the state where you retire or where one of your children gets a divorce.

Most lay people do not (and perhaps *cannot*) know the intricacies of marriage and divorce law in their own state, much less in the several states where their children may live.

Also, the laws of common-law marriage can impact an estate plan; again, each state's statutes are different.

Add to these unknown quantities the laws pertaining to support for children born out of wedlock, and you can readily see that created human relationships can wreck havoc with an estate plan that dares to ignore the many elements that may impact it.

So, let's not ignore them.

Let's be as knowledgeable as possible, but let's arm ourselves against the unknown and against the winds of change that could sweep away even the best laid plan.

In my judgment, the greatest estate planning mistakes made in regard to marriage, are these:

1. Perhaps the most common one is made by married couples who suppose that "my spouse gets everything" and consequently fail to effect a plan. In many states, a person dying without a will and without other provisions for property distribution, leaves *part* to spouse and *part* to children.

The supposition on which the "spouse-gets-everything" plan is founded is, therefore, completely incorrect. It is wrong.

Because the law may leave part to children, those who plan their estates with the "spouse-gets-everything" belief ... initiate their plan from a flawed premise.

The "part-to-children" facet of state laws often present a surprise to the surviving spouse. Perhaps "shock" is a better term. In every case that has come to my attention, the surviving spouse has been shocked and appalled to learn that he or she must share the estate with the children.

Then questions pertaining to the children's age come into play. If they are minors, the court may order that a separate financial guardian must be appointed to watch over the children's inheritance.

Again, the surviving parent views this development with traumatized shock. He or she usually cannot believe that the court would appoint anyone else to look over his shoulder and to be sure that the children's best interests are served.

"Why would I need anyone else to tell me how to spend my late husband's estate on my children?" is a common reaction.

If, on the other hand, the children are adults, the children may, often after some debate, decide to sign waivers that give up their right to the inheritance in favor of their surviving parent.

Often adult children are willing to sign such waivers that surrender their rights.

Now the complex part comes into play.

Under certain circumstances, a Gen II *in-law* could be required to sign the waiver before the Gen I parent can own the entire estate. Most of the people I meet with would not want to be put into a position where they would need to ask their son-in-law for "their" inheritance.

When one parent dies with a "spouse-gets-everything" assumption, three different persons may be required to sign before the surviving parent may act; they are:

    a. Minor children's financial guardian

    b. Adult children

    c. Adult children's spouses

2. The second biggest mistake is, I think, the failure, by couples who have a taxable estate, to divide the estate into two separate ownerships. This failure can impose an additional tax of as much as *$235,000* on the family.

3. When planning the distribution of an estate to children, most planners fail to take their *in-laws* into consideration. They fail to realize that a substantial portion of their estate can quite easily wind up in the hands of in-laws.

4. When marrying, particularly for the second time, planners fail to properly plan the estates so that *each* partner *and* the heirs receive appropriate care.

5. Parents fail to plan for the possibility of *divorce* in their children's lives.

Ignore these five estate planning mistakes at your peril. In our estate planning practice, we see all of them daily. Fortunately, all of them can be avoided with informed and disciplined planning.

State laws, by such means as the "widow's election," have made efforts to protect spouses from inheritance losses, but all of these means can be, under certain circumstances, purposefully or accidentally, circumvented.

The Bypass Trust, the QTIP Trust, the Life Insurance Trust, Premarital Agreements and the Living Revocable Trust can help spouses to plan properly. All of these are discussed at length in other chapters.

THE THREE SECRET WORDS OF ESTATE PLANNING

Accidental disinheritance happens. People who were not the intended beneficiaries of an estate often end up with all or part of it through divorce or other family circumstances.

To prevent a son-in-law from inheriting your money, use the three secret words of estate planning, namely:

"ONLY MY ISSUE"

Your "issue" means your children, grandchildren and great-grandchildren. It very narrowly limits those who can benefit from your estate. Only those in your bloodline qualify for inheritance.

If you create an irrevocable trust ... a not-revocable trust ... and you state in that trust that it is to benefit "only my issue," you prevent your money from ever going to an unintended beneficiary.

In case you want adopted children to benefit, you may expand on the three secret words. You may want to say, "Only my issue ... or legally adopted children of myself and my issue ..."

The three secret words of estate planning are extremely valuable. You may want to use them. Consider them carefully and use them with precision and accuracy.

THE TWO BACK-UP WORDS TO INSURE YOUR TRUST

In the historic Washington, DC suburb of Manassas, VA, a physician and his wife attended one of my estate planning seminars and, after the seminar, asked if they could meet with me.

He was about 60 years old and she was 15 years younger.

He explained, "In addition to my practice, I have invested in a pathology lab that has done exceedingly well."

When he mentioned the name of the lab, I knew of its tremendous growth record ... and I knew that its personnel and facilities now filled three 12-story buildings near my home.

"My stock in the lab is now worth over $4 million," he said.

"Our problem," his wife joined in, "is that our only heir is my daughter ... and we are worried about what might happen to the inheritance if she got it."

"Does she have a problem?" I asked.

"Well, you see, we are not very happy with her religion," the doctor said.

"That's why we came to see you," his wife continued. "My daughter joined a very different religion ... actually, it is a cult ... than we hold ... and she gives all her money to it."

The doctor explained, "Many of the religion's adherents have taken a vow of poverty; they have promised to give everything they own to the religious leaders. We think, probably, she has signed such a vow."

The wife added, "We are sure that she would give any inheritance that she receives from us to the religion and we don't like that idea at all."

"Can one of those trusts that you discussed in the seminar help us?" the doctor asked.

To be sure that I understood their position clearly, I asked, "You do *not* want to totally disinherit her, do you?"

"Oh, no," the doctor said. "We love her dearly. We just don't have any appreciation for her religion."

I explained to them that we could create a trust that would pay only specified benefits to the daughter. With such a trust, the parents could be sure that the principal of the trust, the main body of money, went to the parents' favored people or causes at the daughter's death.

"We call this The Safety Net Trust, the SNT," I said. "The Safety Net Trust can be so worded that no one else but your intended beneficiary can benefit from it. You might want, for example, to give her a stream of income from the trust.

"You can order your trustee to give her a stream of income for life, if that is what you desire."

70

"What if she gave some of the income to the cult?" the woman asked.

"You risk the chance that she might give a portion of that stream of income to the religion," I said. "In no way can you absolutely protect every dime.

"You could protect the principal, the body of money, from being transferred to anyone or anything of which you disapproved."

While the doctor and his wife mulled over my suggestions, I thought to myself, "If these religious leaders have as much power over the daughter as some apparently do, they might present her with a legal paper called An Assignment of Interest. If they persuade her to sign it, they could have the stream of income assigned, or diverted, directly to them.

"If they succeeded in persuading her to sign an Assignment of Interest, they would receive the stream of income for her entire life, whether or not she continued as a devotee of the religion."

I said to the couple, "Let's be extra sure that the stream of income always goes directly to your daughter. Let's guarantee that it is never diverted to the religious leaders or to anyone else. I suggest that we put two precious words into the trust that will forbid any assignment of interest."

Then, I told them the words we would use:
"NOT ASSIGNABLE"

"By stating that the stream of income is not assignable, we will be instructing your corporate trustee to ignore any assignment of interest. We will be telling the bank trust department that it cannot, even if so instructed by your daughter, assign the stream of income to anyone else.

"With these two back-up words, you can rest assured that no one will ever get direct access to the stream of income."

Both the doctor and his wife expressed relief that they did have an option. For the first time, they realized they could, indeed, benefit their daughter and conserve the estate.

Until now, they considered it an "either-or" proposition. They assumed they could either benefit daughter and let her give it to the cult ... or they could deny the daughter anything and be assured that the disliked religion would never benefit from their estate.

Now, they understood that the Safety Net Trust could benefit the daughter ... and ... deny the cult any of their money.

Since that encounter, we have made these two words our standard fare and as a regular feature of our estate plans; we encourage the use of the two back-up words, "Not Assignable."

All of the problems listed in this chapter can be addressed by the judicious use of the SNT. You can avoid in-law inheritors and "step" inheritance. You can prevent the different state marital laws from upsetting your plan.

Finally, you can be sure that your heir does not leave your money to some unwanted person or cause.

FUN QUIZ

CHAPTERS ONE THROUGH SIX

1. T F   The "three secret words" of estate planning are "We want ours."

2. T F   If the trust says that benefits are "not assignable," the trustee cannot give a beneficiary's money to anyone else.

3. T F   To use the Bypass Trust most effectively, each married partner should own part of the estate.

4. T F   A trust can benefit a class of people.

5. T F   At death of the surviving parent, assets pass from the Bypass Trust into the Safety Net Trust.

6. T F   The Bypass trust can be funded with the GSTT exemption amount.

7. T F   With 8 grandchildren, the farmer can use his GSTT exemption 8 times.

8. T F   Income from a QTIP Trust is subject to income tax.

9. T F   A trustee owns assets "for benefit of" others.

10. T F   If one has a Living Revocable Trust, he doesn't need a will.

Test answers are shown on Page 218.

CHAPTER SEVEN

STIFFING THE IRS

As a person who spends over 200 days per year on the road conducting seminars and personal estate plans, I take many of my meals in restaurants, cafes, cafeterias and eateries of all kinds.

There I am served by waiters and waitresses who, for much of their livelihood, depend on the tips left them by the customers.

Like most other regular travelers, I greatly appreciate the job that most of these servers do. Many of them work long and inconvenient hours in order to make the lives of the traveling public easier. Generally, they serve with a smile and focus on the needs of their customers.

Like most of the traveling public, I am all too happy to leave a reasonable tip on the table when my meal is finished. Over the years, I have eaten thousands of meals on the road and, with only two exceptions, have been happy to leave a tip.

However, on those two occasions, I received such poor service that I stiffed the server. (Getting "stiffed" is the common parlance among service personnel to describe a service event wherein they receive no tip.) Feeling that I had received such slovenly service, I left no tip on the table.

I stiffed the server.

TIPPING THE IRS ON INCOME TAX
Every year, millions of Americans leave financial tips for the IRS. In addition to the taxes that they justly owe, millions of taxpayers add a tip to their tax.

Having conducted the personal estate plan for over 4,000 families, I sometimes need to ask a counselee how much tax he or she is paying ... and many times I hear the answer, "Oh! I got money back this year."

Of course, counselees mean by this statement, they overpaid their income tax for the year by a substantial amount and, when calculating their tax, they or their accountants were able to tell the government to send them a check for the amount overpaid.

Indeed, many taxpayers plan their financial situation in a manner that guarantees that they overpay their taxes each year so that they will always "get some back." Many families actually plan their purchases so that they will have money to buy luxuries with the money the government "pays them back."

Little do they realize that they have actually provided the IRS with an interest-free loan for as much as eighteen months at a time and that their "money back" is only a non-interest-bearing return of the principal they have loaned the government.

Julian Block, a self-described, "... former IRS investigator and a tax attorney for the past 30 years ..." said, in the February 1997 Readers Digest that the average taxpayer overpaid income taxes in the amount of $1,240 in 1996. With the average citizen owing nearly $2,000 in credit-card debt at an interest rate of about 20 percent, it is easy to see that taxpayers are actually loaning the government about $1,000 per year on a year-long basis while simultaneously paying $400 in credit-card fees and interest.

The average taxpayer is tipping the IRS about $200 per year in overpayment of income taxes.

Americans should stop these interest-free loans.

They should stiff the IRS.

USING THE ANNUAL EXCLUSION PROPERLY

In Harrisonburg, Virginia, I work with Mr. Merv Webb, Vice President of the Rockingham Memorial Hospital. For several years, I have conducted seminars in behalf of the hospital.

One day, a local resident came in and told me about her mother who lived in another state. She said, "Mother is 87 and there are only the two of us girls, her daughters."

She continued, "Mother has about $4 million worth of pine lands and has never given us any of it. Can Mother, somehow, give us some of the assets ... and get those assets out of her taxable estate? Can she give us those $10,000 gifts that you discussed in the seminar?"

Of course, the answer is a resounding, "Yes."

Mother can give each of the daughters her annual exclusion gift of $10,000 each year. The gift does not have to be a gift of green money. It can be white money. It can be a deed or a share in a partnership, a limited liability company or a corporation.

Our usual recommendation is that a parent create a limited partnership ... and, then, proceed to give limited partnership shares equal to the annual exclusion amount of $10,000 to all heirs each year.

When my counselee left, I had the impression that she would, with all alacrity, implement my advice.

The tragedy is that this approach was not adopted many years previous so that scores of $10,000 annual exclusion gifts could have been transferred.

By waiting until she was eighty-seven years of age to start making gifts, the mother provided a very generous cash tip to the IRS.

USING THE LIFETIME EXEMPTION PROPERLY

While many feel the convenience and the good feeling they experience when receiving their refund check is worth the money they lend the IRS on their income tax, few realize how much they are tipping the IRS in transfer taxes.

With the rapid rise in the sizes of millions of estates, America has more people who are paying estate taxes than at any time in history. Several years ago, researchers determined that Americans are in the process of leaving their heirs and the IRS about $8 trillion (with a T).

However, those calculations were posited when the stock market was about half as high as it is today. As I write these words in a hotel room, I am watching the television out of one eye and seeing that the Dow Jones Average passes 6,600 for the first time today.

It has doubled since the $8 trillion estimate was made.

Yet, every day, my associates and I work with people who have an estate plan designed to tip the IRS.

If a married couple's estate is worth $1.2 million or more ... and if they have not provided for a Bypass Trust in their plan, they are "planning" to tip the IRS $235,000 at the second death.

Yes, I said $235,000.

We think that people should cease tipping the IRS these extravagant and needless amounts.

We believe that taxpayers have paid enough tax and that they should not reward the IRS with these additional tips.

We want to help people cease tipping the IRS.

We want to teach people to stiff the IRS.

Is stiffing the IRS illegal?

Not at all!

Stiffing the IRS is *not* tax evasion. It barely counts as genuine tax avoidance. It is really only refusing to provide the IRS with beneficent bonus tips.

I do not practice tax evasion and I do not teach it.

I teach and practice tax avoidance.

I teach and practice how to stiff the IRS.

Pray tell, what has the IRS done to deserve these tips? Has it served our nation well? Has it provided the citizens of the country with a legitimate service?

Its very name is a travesty; indeed, it is a contradiction of terms ... an oxymoron. Tax collectors provide no service. Rather, the IRS bullies the citizens, frightening them into overpaying their taxes.

Each year, during the tax season, the IRS public relations flacks issue several press releases regarding tax evaders and the severe treatment they have received at the hands of the judicial system.

Timed to hit the newspapers during the "tax season," these press releases are designed to frighten people into being overly cautious in taking their legitimate tax deductions. They are created to assure the

IRS that many citizens will be sure that they tip the IRS to be sure they have paid enough taxes.

When a citizen makes a call to the IRS, he cannot depend on the answer to his question. If he implements the answer and calculates his taxes according to it, IRS may disallow the return. In other words, the advice you receive from the IRS is worthless.

Grover Norquest, President of Americans for Tax Reform serves on one of the IRS commissions. At one of the commission meetings, he asked the question of the IRS management, "You have 120,000 employees. How many of them were fired this year for being rude or abusive to taxpayers?"

When I heard him tell the story on January 8, 1997, he said, "I am still waiting for an answer."

By the way, have you ever heard an IRS agent call you a "citizen?"

No Way !

To the IRS, you are not a citizen; you are a "taxpayer."

Read IRS literature; you will not find a single citation referring to Americans as "citizens." To the IRS, you have two functions and two functions only ... to pay taxes and to tip the IRS.

So far they have not acknowledged that there exist any citizen rights.

Recently a government study by the General Accounting Office found that about one half of the calls to the IRS actually get answered. Only about half even get a voice on the telephone; not to mention those that refer the caller to some other number or give false or misleading information.

I ask you, could you run your business profitably if you answered only half of the telephone calls that came in?

Under no circumstances does IRS deserve the bonuses and tips that American citizens are generously granting them.

USING THE GENERATION SKIP

Families are legally entitled to hold on to limited amounts of their money for two or three generations without payment of estate taxes. By using a generation skip, or genskip, a family can delay the payment of tax on substantial amounts of money. Properly executed, the generation skip can delay tax on $1 million per donor for as much as, in many cases, 25 years.

Few Americans take advantage of this excellent estate planing strategy. Through ignorance of the law and fear of the IRS, people fail to take advantage of generation skipping tactics; hence, they tip the IRS.

USING CHARITABLE TRUSTS

When presented with the option of using a charitable trust that pays income to family members for a period of time prior to the asset's going to charity, many Americans fear the IRS and, instead of providing for their charitable causes, they tip the IRS.

One New York accountant demurred when a development executive at Dowling College, presented the charitable trust option. The accountant decided instead to pay the tax.

After the deal was done, the accountant was asked why he refused to use the charitable trust. The accountant replied, "I understand taxes. I don't understand charitable trusts. So, I just paid the taxes."

Instead of going to the books or to some expert and learning more about the marvelous tax avoidance measures inherent in charitable trusts, the accountant decided it would be easier to give the IRS a bonus. He led his client to give the IRS a nice tip.

As seen by this example, not only are citizens tipping the IRS; many professional people who should indeed understand the various means of legal tax avoidance, are also providing the IRS with abundant bonus tax payments. They are tipping the IRS.

USING THE ESTATE SHRINK

Millions of American families possess assets that could be "shrunk" for estate tax purposes. Farmers, land owners and business owners are all prime candidates for the estate shrink.

Unfortunately, few are aware of this excellent estate planning device; hence, they do not use it.

An estate that consists, to a large degree, of land or business interests, can generally be shrunk by about one fourth, reducing the taxable estate and removing assets from the top estate tax rate.

Many advisors are not aware that such a mechanism exists; or, they are afraid to use it less IRS identify them as audit targets. Therefore they design plans that cause their clients to pay more taxes, to tip the IRS.

I was totally shocked recently when conducting the personal estate plan for an Iowa business woman whose late husband had been a farmer. With an estate of about $1.5 million, she had a tremendous estate tax problem.

She told me that she had expressed to her lawyer her desire to give some of the land to her two daughters.

Expecting to hear that he showed her how to use the Family Limited Partnership and the Estate Shrink, I listened more carefully.

Instead she reached into her valise and pulled out a deed that he had prepared. The deed gave each daughter a sliver of land. It transferred a tiny bit of land. This is an amateurish strategy in and of itself because it chops up the land and makes it have a lower market value.

His greater omission was that he failed to show his client how she could shrink the estate for tax purposes by adopting that strategy.

I was especially dismayed because he was an Iowa attorney; he lived and practiced in a state where great numbers of people could use the tax advantage permitted by shrinking the estate.

From all appearances, he is providing all his clients a similar low level of professional service.

Even when advisors show their clients how to shrink the estate, many people are hesitant to follow through. Recently, I met with a retired banker and his wife to help them with their estate plan.

Owning considerable land, they had been advised to adopt the shrink strategy.

"But," the banker admitted, "I just never got around to implementing the lawyer's advice."

When your advisors give you good advice, follow through and implement their ideas.

PURCHASING LIFE INSURANCE

Life insurance can be a valuable estate planning technique; but unfortunately, our nation has an industry that is more concerned with the provision of life insurance than it is with optimally serving the clients.

More times than I can count, counselees have come in to me for estate planning and have shown me that they had one planning document, a life insurance policy.

Immediately I know who has been doing their estate planning, a life insurance agent.

I have no quarrel with the judicious use of life insurance in an estate plan; but most life insurance agents are not knowledgeable of tax avoidance procedures. Instead of helping the client avoid taxes, the life insurance industry has, for the most part, merely shown the client how to prepay the tax by purchasing large life insurance policies.

By failing to first show the client how to avoid taxes, life insurance agents are merely providing the IRS with maximum tax income. They are helping their client tip the IRS.

STOP TIPPING THE IRS

By using several of the devices and strategies in this book, you can cease the generous tips you may be providing the IRS.

Pay your just taxes; but stop tipping the IRS.

FUN QUIZ

CHAPTERS ONE THROUGH SEVEN

1. T F   The IRS pays a high interest rate on withheld taxes.

2. T F   Shrinking the estate can save taxes.

3. T F   The $600,000 lifetime exemption can be used during life or at death.

4. T F   The annual exclusion from gift taxes is $10,000.

5. T F   IRS agents are severely disciplined for being rude or abusive to taxpayers.

6. T F   A Limited Partner is one who has equal voting rights.

7. T F   A Crummey Trust "ain't so crummy."

8. T F   "With right of survivorship" refers to living 100 years.

9. T F   Ninety-one is a good age for a multi-millionaire to begin making annual exclusion gifts.

10. T F   Only checks made out to the IRS qualify as annual exclusion gifts.

Test answers are shown on Page 219.

CHAPTER EIGHT

THE TAX LABYRINTH

As our system of state, federal and local governments has grown, and as politicians of different persuasions have held the reins of power for various intervals, our tax laws have become an interconnected maze through which an ordinary citizen dare not venture without the very best professional advice.

When dealing with estate planning, we must hurdle many different kinds of tax. The neophyte is not prepared for battle. All of these taxes can impinge, in one way or another, on the estate planning process.

    Federal capital gains tax
    Federal estate tax
    Federal excise tax
    Federal gift tax
    Federal income tax
    Generation Skipping Transfer Tax
    State capital gains tax
    State estate tax
    State gift tax
    State income tax
    State inheritance tax

Obviously, this labyrinth constitutes a maze through which only the most well trained and experienced professional person can pilot. Let's take a look at these taxes and try to make sense of them individually and collectively.

FEDERAL INCOME TAX

All of us are cognizant of our responsibility to pay federal income tax on each year's earnings. Most of us, however, are not familiar with the fact that a deceased person's estate may be required to pay federal income tax on the person's income earned during the portion of the year that he or she lived.

If a person lives for one half a year, for example, and earns income, his executor or trustee must be sure that income tax is paid on the income earned in that part of the year that the decedent lived. Many executors are surprised to learn that they must calculate the decedent's income for the partial year and must pay tax on it.

The decedent may have had substantial taxes withheld from his wages or may have paid quarterly taxes before death. The Executor will want to check these payments to know precisely how much has been prepaid.

In addition, the executor should check the decedent's income tax returns for the past three years ... and be sure that the income tax has been paid before making final distribution to the heirs.

The stories are legion about executors who paid out all the estate to heirs ... and who, subsequently, received a tax bill for which they were personally responsible.

If the decedent had a IRA, 401k, 403b or other deferred pension plan, the executor may need to pay income tax on those proceeds before they are disbursed to heirs.

All these tax decisions can become quite complicated. Consequently, many executors and trustees seek the help of their Certified Public Accountant to be sure that all taxes are paid.

In some instances, it may be a good idea to keep some money in reserve, just in case the IRS audits a tax return and decides that more tax is owed. Having about three and one half years, under non-fraudulent rules, to audit the return, IRS may send a bill for additional taxes. It may be wise to retain some funds for that period of time. After that period, it is generally safe to disburse to the heirs.

FEDERAL ESTATE AND GIFT TAX

When a person dies in possession of a taxable estate, the executor or trustee must file a Form 706 Federal Estate Tax Return and must pay any tax due. The estate may be valued either at the time of death ... or within six months of death.

In a "Bull Market," it is smart to value the estate as of the date of death. If, on the other hand, the value of the estate is decreasing, it may be better to value at the six-month mark.

Gifts to human beings made during your life are subject to federal gift tax. If you give one person more than $10,000 in any one calendar year, you must file a Form 709 Federal Gift Tax Return and pay any tax due.

For all practical purposes, the tax on gifts and on estates is the same amount. The 1976 tax law changed the taxes from being two different taxes and "unified" them. The two taxes are sometimes called "the unified tax." The $192,800 tax credit on the $600,000 exemption is sometimes called "the unified tax credit."

Thus, if a person uses up $300,000 of his $600,000 lifetime exemption by making gifts during life, he has only $300,000 left to use at death. He is said to have used up part of his $192,800 "unified credit."

Every asset belonging to the deceased, whether it is green money or white money is subject to federal estate tax. All real estate, collectibles, stocks, bonds, corporate shares and all cash must be totaled up to ascertain the taxable estate.

The tax is not a small one. It starts at thirty-seven percent on the first dollar above $600,000 ... and rises to as much as fifty-five percent.

Typical Gift and Estate Tax Bites

Estate of $ 750,000	$ 56,000
Estate of $1,000,000	$ 153,000
Estate of $2,000,000	$ 588,000
Estate of $3,000,000	$1,098,000

As you are aware, most people never think about the federal estate tax bite. Those who do consider it, often seem to think that nothing can be done about it. To a large degree, federal estate tax is an "optional" tax. With good planning, many families can greatly reduce their federal gift and estate tax obligation.

There are *four* basic ways to avoid federal estate tax. An intelligent use of the four can greatly reduce taxes. To arrive at the ability to use the four methods intelligently, a person needs to understand all four and their interrelationships. The four avoidance procedures are:

1. The Spousal Rule: There is no tax on spousal transfers, whether in life, by gift, or at death, by legacy. You can give any amount of money to your spouse and pay no federal gift tax. Likewise, you can leave any amount to your spouse, as a legacy, and pay no federal estate tax.

2. The Lifetime Exemption Rule: Each person has a lifetime exemption from estate taxation of $600,000. This exemption may be used during life ... or at death. But not at both. As previously stated, one might use part of the exemption during life; part at death.

3. The Annual Exclusion Rule: Each donor can give $10,000 to as many recipients each year as he chooses. If he gives more than $10,000 to one individual, he must file a Form 709, Federal Gift Tax Return, show the amount of the gift and, perhaps, pay tax.

4. The Charitable Rule: There is no federal gift or estate tax on gifts made to legitimate charitable organizations.

An intelligent use of these means of avoiding federal estate tax can save families thousands ... or hundreds of thousands ... of dollars.

Here is the way to learn the application of these rules.
1. We get the first one ... and get to keep it.
2. Then, we get the second one ... and get to keep it.
3. Then, we get the third one ... and get to keep it.
4. We then get the fourth one.
To review:
1. We get the spousal rule ... and get to keep it.
2. We get the $600,000 lifetime exemption rule
   ... and get to keep it.
3. We get the $10,000 annual exclusion rule
   ... and get to keep it.
4. We get the charitable rule.

In our estate planning practice, we find that many people know a little bit about this set of rules. They generally do not know how to apply them in any rational manner.

Therefore, you need to learn the four-tier method as shown above. With this knowledge, you will know that the use of the spousal rule does not prevent you from using the lifetime exemption rule.

Likewise, the use of the $600,000 lifetime exemption does not prevent you from using the annual exclusions of $10,000. The annual exclusions do not subtract from the $600,000. You get both.

The $10,000 annual exclusion rule dies with you; so the only way to use it is to do so during life.

Very few people know that they can use the $600,000 lifetime exemption during life. In some cases, it is wise to use this means of tax avoidance during life.

In addition to those rules, the tax community has come up with some other ways to avoid tax. Perhaps the greatest tax saver is the one commonly known as the Bypass Trust. It is also known as the A/B Trust, The Credit Shelter Trust, The Credit Trust, etc. Generally, I refer to it as the Bypass.

By using the Bypass Trust, a married couple can be sure that each of them uses his *and* her $600,000 lifetime exemption for a total exemption of $1.2 million. This approach can result in a tax savings of as much as $235,000.

Annual gifts, made to people or trusts, can substantially reduce the taxable estate and can save as much as $5,500 each time a gift of $10,000 is made.

When using a grandchildren's trust as the object of giving, the married couple with four grandchildren could, for example, give both of their $600,000 exemptions and $80,000 per year in annual exclusion gifts. The first year they could give $1,280,000 to the trust for benefit of (FBO) grandchildren.

Here's how this would work:

1. Grandfather gives his $600,000 lifetime exemption.
2. Grandmother gives her $600,000 lifetime exemption.

3. Grandfather gives four $10,000 annual exclusion gifts for a total of $40,000.

4. Grandmother gives four $10,000 annual exclusion gifts for a total of $40,000.

Altogether, the two grandparents have given $1,280,000 in one year with absolutely no tax liability.

Having used their $600,000 lifetime exemptions in that year, they never have the benefit of the lifetime exemption again.

The $10,000 annual exclusion gift is a renewable asset. It may be used over and over again.

Assuming that their number of grandchildren remained the same, the two grandparents could continue their $10,000 annual exclusion gifts as long as they live. Their total annual exclusion gift would amount to $80,000 each year.

If they started this regimen while they were still young, they could move a very substantial part of their estate to the grandchildren's trust without taxation.

In our estate planning seminars, we find that few attendees understand the federal gift and estate tax and their exclusions and exemptions. While they are familiar with the $600,000 figure and the $10,000 number, they have little knowledge of the way these avoidance procedures relate to one another.

RE-TAXATION: AN IRS AGENT'S DREAM

Can family assets be subject to estate tax in more than one estate?

Can assets be re-taxed?

Yes. The IRS can tax the assets each time they are passed from one owner to another non-spouse owner.

Suppose you have a great aunt, Margaret Anita Buckingham. You probably just call her Aunt Meg ... Aunt Meg A. Bucks.

Aunt Meg A. Bucks has $10 million.

Her daughter has zero.

Her granddaughter has zero.

Her great-granddaughter has zero.

All the husbands have died.

Aunt Meg A. Bucks dies and leaves everything to her daughter. Of the $10 million estate, IRS gets half.

The daughter is left with $5 million.

Five years later, she dies leaving everything to her daughter.

Does IRS come around and shake hands with the whole family and say, "Well, thank you very much. You folks have already paid tax on this money. Just take a nice vacation and enjoy yourselves."

Of course not. They want more tax.

They take about $2 million leaving the heir with $3 million.

Another five years go by and this heir dies.

IRS wants its tax again. This time the tax is about $1 million, leaving the heir a net of $2 million out of great-grandmother's $10 million estate.

Can we completely avoid this exorbitant taxation?

Not exactly!

But we can ameliorate it by using generation skips.

Each person has a $1 million exemption from generation skip-ping transfer tax (GSTT) and smart families are using their exemptions.

We are showing the generation skip (GenSkip) to every grandparent and great-grandparent who comes to us for estate plan assistance. It is an effective, outstanding estate planning device.

In Annapolis, Maryland, in December of 1991, I was invited to meet with a four-generation family to plan the matriarch's estate. The invitation came from her 70-year-old nephew who had accepted the responsibility of helping his aunt with her financial affairs.

Waiting for the matriarch and her nephew to arrive, the group gathered in her stockbroker's conference room; included in the group were the stockbroker and the stockbrokerage's trust officer, the lady's attorney and her accountant.

At the appointed time, the nephew and his forty-year-old son ushered the matriarch into the room.

A charming and elegant octogenarian, she faced me, shook my hand firmly and said, "Mr. Recer, I do *not* want to pay any more tax. My late husband, who was President of the local college, and I have paid more than our share of taxes."

I assured her that I would make every effort to show the group several tax avoidance procedures.

With an estate of over $2 million, a charitable inclination and with nephews, great-nephews and great-great nephews, she had many opportunities for tax avoidance.

Obviously, the generation skip and charitable trusts were valuable tools in our strategy of tax avoidance. In her case, the matriarch could conduct a double generation skip. She could create a trust for the fourth generation and bring the income and other benefits from the trust back to generations two and three during their lives.

By using the generation skip, we were able to substantially reduce the re-taxation hit that many families experience. While I could not absolutely eliminate the matriarch's tax, I had the pleasure of helping the family greatly reduce it.

STATE DEATH TAXES

State inheritance and estate taxes are broadly described as "death taxes." Some states have an estate tax; some have an inheritance tax and some have no direct tax.

Every state benefits from taxable estates. About two-thirds of the states have a pick-up tax law. By virtue of these pick-up taxes, a state can enjoy participation in the federal estate tax. Using this tax, states can take part of the federal tax levy.

They are generally said to have "no" inheritance tax or estate tax. This really means they take part of the amount that is calculated as federal estate tax. The following states participate in the pick-up tax:

Alabama, Alaska, Arizona, Arkansas, California, Colorado, District of Columbia, Florida, Georgia, Hawaii, Idaho, Illinois, Maine, Minnesota, Missouri, Nevada, New Mexico, North Dakota, Oregon, Rhode Island, South Carolina, Texas, Utah, Vermont, Virginia, Washington, West Virginia, Wisconsin, Wyoming.

The other states impose a state death tax either in the form of an inheritance tax or an estate tax. An inheritance tax is a tax on the assets received by a person. An estate tax is a tax on the assets of the decedent.

The maximum tax in each of those states is:

Connecticut.....	14%	Montana.....	32%
Delaware.....	16%	Nebraska.....	18%
Indiana.....	15%	New Hampshire.....	15%
Iowa.....	15%	New Jersey.....	16%
Kansas.....	15%	New York.....	21%
Kentucky.....	16%	North Carolina.....	17%
Louisiana......	10%	Ohio.....	7%
Maryland.....	10%	Oklahoma.....	15%
Massachusetts.....	16%	Pennsylvania.....	15%
Michigan.....	17%	South Dakota.....	30%
Mississippi.....	16%	Tennessee.....	13%

The state death tax is not "in addition to" the federal estate tax because the federal law allows an offset for the payment of state death taxes. The tax is difficult for the layman to calculate. If you need specific calculations on the tax due, you would be wise to depend on your Certified Public Accountant.

Many states have designated different classes of beneficiaries. Classes of people most closely related to the decedent are, for the most part, taxed at a lower rate than are more distant relatives or heirs.

For example, in Maryland, the state classifies those people in the direct ancestral line as lineal descendants. For those directly above and directly below in the family tree, the lineal descendants, the state inheritance tax is only one percent.

The tax is not onerous when assets go to mother, father, children, grandchildren and great-grandchildren.

For collateral descendants, uncles, aunts, cousins, etc., the Maryland inheritance tax is ten percent.

Actually, Maryland's lineal and collateral law is fairly simple when compared to some of the other states.

To completely understand your state's death tax and its calculation may be a next-to-impossible task. To know your state and the states where your heirs live may cross the threshold of impossibility.

The key points to remember are that state death taxes can greatly add to a family's tax burden ... and that the use of the four means of federal tax avoidance, generally apply to state death taxes as well.

State death taxes serve as an exclamation point ... telling us to use the federal tax avoidance rules intelligently.

CAPITAL GAINS TAX

Capital gains tax is levied by the federal government and by many state governments.

The capital gains tax is actually an income tax applied to capital gains ... or income tax on the gain.

With federal capital gains tax rates as high as 20% ... and with many states adding on a substantial tax, many people pay as much as one third of their realized gain in state and federal capital gains taxes.

When an owned asset appreciates in value, it has a gain. When that asset is sold at a higher price than its purchase price, the taxpayer is said to have a *realized gain*. It is the realized gain that triggers the capital gains tax.

A key issue in calculating this tax is a value known as "basis." Basis is, with some minor exceptions, broadly defined as "What you paid for the asset."

To calculate the realized gain ... and calculate the capital gains tax, you must know your basis. Subtract the basis from the sales price to find the realized gain. If you paid a commission on the sale, subtract that figure from the gain and, thus, come up with your net realized gain.

Apply the capital gains tax rate to the net realized gain to ascertain the tax. Don't forget that you may be required to pay both federal and state capital gains tax.

If, for example, you bought a stock for $100 in 1975 and its value increased at 7.2% per year for 20 years, it would have been worth

$400 by 1995 ... and you would have, in 1995, an unrealized capital gain of $300.

If you sold at the $400 figure, you would have realized a capital gain of $300 ... and that gain would have been subject to the tax. Remember, as long as you didn't sell, you have not realized a capital gain ... hence, you have not experienced a taxable event.

To recap this scene, let's use a table:

Selling Price	$400
Basis	$100
Realized Gain	$300

A taxable event transpires when you sell and realize a gain.

Now let's turn to the capital gains tax implications for gifts and legacies. We will calculate the tax implications if you *gave* a gift; then we will calculate the tax implications if you died and left a *legacy* of an appreciated asset.

If, instead of selling the stock in 1995 for $400, you gave the stock to your cousin and he immediately sold it, the realized gain would be the same and the tax would be the same because your basis carried over to him. This is called "carry-over" basis ... and is the operative concept when making gifts.

Our table for the sale when cousin sells the gift is identical to the one above.

Selling price	$400
Basis	$100
Realized gain	$300

Gift equals carry-over basis.

If, on the other hand, you died in 1995 and left the stock to your cousin who immediately sold it at the $400 figure, the basis is different. In the case of transfers at death, the basis is "stepped up" to the fair market value at time of death.

If you paid $100 and died and left it to your cousin in 1995 when it was worth $400, his basis is stepped up to the $400 figure. If he sells the next day for that price, he pays no capital gains tax because his basis and his selling price is the same. He has not realized a capital gain so he pays no tax.

Our table for cousin's sale of a legacy looks like this.

Selling price	$400
Basis	$400
Realized gain	$000

Die equals stepped-up basis.

To repeat: Gift equals carry-over basis. Die equals stepped-up basis.

When the average taxpayer first learns the difference in carry-over basis and stepped-up basis, he usually says,

"Eureka, don't ever give anything away
during life. Wait until death and get
a stepped-up basis."

A more judicious look at the problem, however, shows that you should be careful that you do not over value this "step up" in basis. Some planners very adroitly avoid the 35% capital gains tax only to pay 55% estate tax on the same asset. Don't "save" capital gains tax only to pay more estate tax.

What is the answer?

There is no general answer. Each of us must view our own assets and determine if and when gifts during life will make more sense than legacies at death. It is complex because both capital gains tax and estate tax must be counter-balanced.

We must decide whether or not heirs are ready for gifts ... or whether we are ready to make gifts to a trust for the heirs.

If you have a highly taxable estate, you would be wise to work with your tax advisor to create a plan that uses this means of tax avoidance in an intelligent manner.

HOW TRUSTS ARE TAXED

From time to time, seminar attendees or counselees will raise an objection to trusts because they say,

"I heard that trusts pay far more
taxes than individuals do."

Here is a short effort to set the record straight on the two kinds of trusts about which I get this question the most: the Living Revocable Trust and the Safety Net Trust.

Because the Living Revocable Trust (LRT) can be completely revoked at any time, the IRS doesn't even want to know about it. The IRS wants you to pay your taxes and the LRT's taxes on only one form. You pay all taxes on both your income and on the trust's income on your tax form and you use your social security number as the identification number. The LRT is *not* a taxpayer.

The Safety Net Trust (SNT), or Spendthrift Trust (ST), on the other hand, *is* a taxpayer. Because it is an irrevocable trust, a not-revocable trust, its Trustee *does* apply for a tax identification number and *does* file an income tax return each year.

The Trustee may ... or may not... pay tax for the SNT in a given year; but an income tax return is filed each year.

If the SNT earns income and pays out all the income to beneficiaries, it files a return and says to the IRS, "I made income; but I paid it all out. I had *no net income* therefore, I owe *no* taxes."

If, on the other hand, the SNT earns and keeps the income in a given year, it will, most probably, pay tax. The tax is no major problem if the trust earns less than $7,500. However, for all income in excess of that figure, the trust pays at the maximum federal income tax rate, currently 39.6%.

If the purpose of the SNT is to build a college fund for children or grandchildren, it will, most likely, be invested in growth stocks and will not realize much income. Growth is a capital gain ... and when the gain is not realized ... when nothing is sold... there is no tax.

There are many ways for a trust to avoid the high tax rate that so many people fear. Do not let the tax issue deter you from establishing a Safety Net Trust. Savvy investment counselors and accountants can show you how to minimize taxes.

GENERATION-SKIPPING TRANSFER TAX

In addition to the concerns you have about federal estate tax ... and about state and local estate and inheritance taxes, you need to know about another transfer tax which is called "Generation Skipping Transfer Tax (GSTT)."

Because of greater American longevity, many families have four generations living at one time; even five generations are not rare.

Government lawmakers believe that the federal government deserves its tax each time one generation dies.

If a person owning a large taxable estate were to "skip" down one or two generations, giving or leaving his estate to grandchildren or great-grandchildren ... or to trusts for their benefit, he would avoid one or two levels of taxation.

In the minds of federal officials, this strategy would deny the government its tax ... or would substantially delay the imposition of the tax.

Recognizing that people might adopt such a strategy ... and calculating that the government might "lose" substantial tax revenues, federal officials created another tax which applies to "skips," the Generation Skipping Transfer Tax.

To discourage skips, the tax was set at an unbelievably high level. It is so high that one noted writer has calculated the tax at 140%. That's right: *one hundred and forty percent.*

However, the law allows an exemption of $1 million from GSTT. A grandmother can give her grandchildren as much as $1 million, in life or at death ... or in a combination of lifetime and at-death transfers ... and pay no GSTT. The $1 million is counted by the grandmother; not by the grandchildren. It is not $1 million per grandchild.

Suppose that a grandmother had eight grandchildren and that she wanted to optimize her skipping powers. To avoid both GSTT and the federal estate tax (FET), she would need to do as follows:

Year 1: Give $10,000 to each grandchild...	$ 80,000
Year 2: Give $10,000 to each grandchild...	$ 80,000
Year 3: Give $10,000 to each grandchild...	$ 80,000
Year 4: Give $10,000 to each grandchild...	$ 80,000
Year 5: Give $10,000 to each grandchild...	$ 80,000
In life or at death, leave her lifetime exemption amount to the grandchildren:	$ 600,000
Total removed from grandmother's estate	$1,000,000
Total federal estate tax	$0,000,000
Total generation skipping transfer tax	$0,000,000

Of course, it would be better to give these gifts to a trust for the grandchildren than to give it to each of them outright.

The rules are complex and you will need your accountant's help; but if you have a highly taxable estate, you may profit by use of your GSTT exemption. You may want to skip one or possibly more generations.

HOW MUCH IS THE $600,000 LIFETIME EXEMPTION WORTH NOW?

By virtue of the Economic Recovery Act of 1981, the federal government raised the Lifetime Exemption from federal gift and estate tax to $600,000, effective as of January 1, 1987. The 1981 Act gradually increased the exemption from $225,000 in 1982 to the $600,000 figure at the beginning of 1987.

As I write these words, in the winter of 1996/1997, we are "celebrating" the ten-year anniversary of the $600,000 figure for the Lifetime Exemption. That figure has been the operable number for a decade.

Unfortunately, for taxpayers, the Lifetime Exemption has not been changed by statue since its 1987 increase.

However, the realities of the marketplace have changed it. When viewed in a market context, the Lifetime Exemption has been substantially reduced since 1987.

To a Dow Jones Industrial Average investor, for example, the Lifetime Exemption is presently worth less than $200,000 in 1987 dollars.

A look at the table on the following page substantiates this claim.

HOW TO DISINHERIT YOUR SON-IN-LAW

DJIA INVESTORS' LIFETIME EXEMPTION

YEAR LAST DAY	DJIA	DJIA % OF 1986 LAST DAY	LIFETIME EXEMPTION IN 1/87 DJIA $
1986	1896	1.00000	$600,000
1987	1939	1.02267	$586,694
1988	2169	1.14398	$524,481
1989	2753	1.45200	$413,222
1990	2634	1.38924	$431,891
1991	3169	1.67141	$358,978
1992	3400	1.79325	$334,588
1993	3493	1.84229	$325,680
1996*	5592	2.94936	$203,433

*Close on 4/15/96

100

FUN QUIZ

CHAPTERS ONE THROUGH EIGHT

1. T F When one has a Living Revocable Trust, he must file a separate federal income tax return for the trust.

2. T F An irrevocable trust is a taxpayer.

3. T F Capital gains tax is a form of estate tax.

4. T F Probate has been known to last many years.

5. T F Generation skipping saves income tax.

6. T F Capital gains tax is owed when one realizes a gain.

7. T F Some states impose a state estate tax.

8. T F If you have living great-grandchildren, you might do a double generation skip.

9. T F The same money can be subjected to federal estate tax more than once.

10. T F If a person lives for only the first six months of the year and earns income while living, his income is subject to income tax.

Test answers are shown on Page 220.

CHAPTER NINE

"PROFESSIONALS" WHO AREN'T

Many "professionals" have no stake in your being able to design an effective estate plan. On the contrary, some have an interest in your plan being outdated, ineffective and inefficient.

Because estate planning is a composite of several kinds of planning, there are often many different "cooks" in the kitchen. Unfortunately, many of those cooks get their recipes from distinct and separate ends of the kitchen.

Often their concoctions are designed with one purpose in mind ... to fatten their wallets; not to provide for the client's nutrition. Be careful whom you let into the kitchen. Be sure they are all reading off the same page of the cookbook, the one that says, "Nutritious Recipes for the Client."

Attorneys:

Attorneys, for example, may have many reasons to want their clients to have a poor estate plan. Please understand that I do not say here, that *all* attorneys have this agenda; but it is quite true that many of them have separate agendas from those of their clients.

The vast majority of attorneys do not like the Living Revocable Trust (LRT). Knowing that this trust saves probate fees, many attorneys are diametrically opposed to its use. Instead of looking out for their clients' financial interest, these lawyers want their clients' estates to go through the expensive probate process.

Many attorneys attend my seminars. In those appearances, I cover a large number of estate planning devices, including the LRT. Generally, I spend about ten percent of the seminar time on the LRT.

Almost universally, lawyers have criticized the seminar as being a "Living Trust Seminar." In other words, they sit through the whole meeting, hear me explain several estate planning devices; but think of only one stratagem, the LRT.

They often attend the seminar looking for something wrong ... and they tend to pounce on the LRT and vociferously to demonstrate their mindless animus for its use.

Many of these lawyers earn part of their living by probating estates; by performing the clerical work involved in transferring assets from the decedent to the heirs. In many cases, lawyers conduct much of this clerical work themselves; and, of course, they charge much more than clerical fees.

On the other hand, some of them pass the work to subordinates or to contract employees who actually perform the work.

In El Paso, Texas, one attorney told me that he charges one thousand dollars for each probate and that he "sells" each of the probate deals to an independent paralegal for one hundred dollars. "She does all the work and I make $900 per case," he bragged to me.

Another reason these lawyers despise the LRT and other sophisticated estate planning devices is that they know a diligent estate planning process requires much earnest mental work. This creative labor often needs to be performed in a tight time-frame.

They also know that a "Sweetheart-Will-Plan" requires no creativity or diligence on their part and is, therefore, easy to draft; in many cases, it already exists on their word processor.

Because it is easy to draft and because all the real work will take place after the client dies ... at a leisurely pace that piles up the legal bills, they love the "Sweetheart Will" approach to estate planning. As you will see in later chapters, Sweetheart Wills are tax land mines.

Speaking of documents on word processors, let me digress for a moment and tell you of a very honest lawyer I met in Potsdam, New York. He was a former state legislator. When he and his wife came to see me for estate planning help, he reported,

"I did many wills in my years in law practice; but, to tell the truth, I didn't know much about

estate planning. But I had a good Form Book.
I had a book that had all the forms of wills in it.
When I needed a specific will, I just went to
the form book and copied it down."

While many consumers would not think it proper for their will to be "copied from a book," they would, in this case, at least, be in the hands of an honest lawyer.

When Mr. Graham Lee, Chief Development Official at the Memorial Hospital of Easton, Maryland, and I were working with one gentleman on his estate plan, he told us that he had decided he wanted a living revocable trust. Having made that decision, he had gone to his attorney to have an LRT drafted.

Admitting that he was not well versed in estate planning, the attorney told the client that he would contact his brother-in-law in Montana who was also an attorney and who had a model living trust document on his word processor.

Evidently the Maryland attorney received an LRT form on a diskette from his brother-in-law and typed in his local client's name to design a living trust.

He then presented the trust and his bill to the client.

The man proudly handed his living trust document to Graham Lee and me when he arrived for our conference.

While I was working with the man, Graham sat in the corner and began to read through the trust. After a while, he brought the trust over to me and pointed out a clause on page twenty-three. It noted that "this trust is governed by the laws of the state of Montana."

Obviously, the Maryland attorney hadn't even read the entire trust that he foisted off on his client. Had he read it, he certainly would have removed "Montana" from the pre-packaged trust document and substituted "Maryland."

This lazy attorney certainly did not serve his client well.

When an attorney excels in law school, he has well learned how to communicate with the Supreme Court Justices of the United States. Law professors are very careful to teach their students how to demonstrate their knowledge to judges.

However, there are no courses in law school on means of communicating with clients. Law school, in no way, prepares a lawyer to communicate with clients. A person can be recognized by his peers as an outstanding attorney and have little ability to communicate with his clients.

While working in Burlington with Rusty Brink, the chief development officer of the Fletcher-Allen (Medical) Foundation in Vermont, I was visited by a businessman. He came to me to design his estate and told me that, five years previously, he had decided to work on his estate plan and had made an appointment with an attorney to plan his $20 million estate.

"But," he continued, "after about five minutes of listening to the attorney explain what I needed to do, *my eyes glazed over.*

"I couldn't understand a word the lawyer said. Everything he said sounded like Greek to me. I walked out and just forgot about doing any estate planning.

"That's been five years ago ... and I still have no estate plan."

By their total misunderstanding of the tax laws and the elements in an estate plan, some attorneys are able to charge their clients more money and to introduce additional tax burdens on people.

In Norfolk, Virginia, while working with Beth Duke, Senior Vice President of The Children's Hospital of the King's Daughters, I was conducting a seminar in early 1997 at the Barry Robinson Center, an affiliate of the Children's Hospital.

At the seminar break, a woman of about seventy-five years approached me and asked for advice. She said that her husband had, for the last few years, exhibited signs of dementia and that his condition had motivated her to seek an attorney's advice.

She explained, "My husband and I owned everything jointly. The attorney advised me to get everything into my name alone."

"That was good advice," I said.

"But the way he did it concerned me," she continued. "He told me to have my husband transfer all his assets to the children ... and then have the children convert the assets to my ownership."

She asked, "What do you think of that approach?"

Shocked at the attorney's recommendation, I nearly slipped and told the woman exactly what I thought.

Realizing that my criticism of the attorney would gain her nothing ... and thinking that it would be better to alleviate her concerns, I said, "Well, that approach accomplished the primary goal. You now own everything in your name only. Correct?"

"Yes," she confirmed, "I own everything."

I told her that there was a much simpler way ... that the attorney could have encouraged her husband to sign a quit claims to her. For the real property (real estate), he could simply sign a Quit-Claim Deed in her favor and this would give everything to her with no tax consequences of any kind.

For joint bank and stock accounts, he could agree to have his name removed from ownership.

Instead, the lawyer's method created two taxable events. When the father gave the assets to the children, that was a taxable event.

Again, when the children gave to their mother, they experienced a taxable event.

She appeared to understand. "My estate exceeds the $600,000 figure; so I have to pay tax don't I?" Then she said, "What do I do now?"

The lawyer, unwisely, had placed assets into an already-taxable estate when he encouraged the children to transfer assets to their mother. This meant that the same assets taxable in the father's and children's estates would also be taxable in the mother's.

IRS had hit the trifecta.

The family's assets would be taxed three times!

To the best of my short-hand calculation during the seminar break, the lawyer had cost the family about one hundred thousand dollars.

The probate establishment, the cabal of lawyers, accountants, insurance salesmen, investment traders, judges and appraisers and government entities, have a great financial interest in your doing everything the wrong way.

Your mistakes are the probate establishment's bread and butter. When you err, they earn. Your errors of omission translate into their years of consumption.

Many members of these professions have conspired to deny you and your fellow Americans of simple, understandable, expeditious and reasonable means of settling the affairs of deceased people.

As masters of obfuscation and circumlocution, they have retained every dilatory, time-consuming method of performing the simplest act. Paid by the hour, they have learned every possible way to do things more slowly.

While the computer has speeded all other forms of paper movement in our society, these professionals have colluded and connived to perform busy work and to charge outrageous fees for their time.

One lawyer inadvertently revealed one of their favorite techniques. He explained to a relative, who then related the explanation to me, of the proper way to submit papers to the court.

Instead of driving down to the court with the papers for four cases in his hand and charging each client the proportionate share of his time and expense for doing so, he said,

> *"The proper way to submit these papers is to figure that it takes two hours to drive from my office to the court house, park, stop at the snack bar, have a cup of coffee with some other lawyers, submit the papers to the recording clerk and return. I charge each client for the two hours' time. In other words, I am able to charge for eight hours of professional time for the two hours work."*

Contrast the legal profession's use of dilatory and duplicative tactics with that of the information industry. In recent years, the cost of communications has dropped dramatically because each company is trying to perform more economically than the competition.

Thanks to this competition, the price of communications has dropped greatly.

But the cost of legal services, based on the hourly rate, has continued to sky rocket.

Recently I received a call from an accountant in Tampa, Florida. He reported that a wealthy man died leaving a behind widow extremely unsophisticated in financial matters. With an estate of more than $20 million, she was savvy enough to know that she needed some kind of an estate plan.

Knowing nothing about legal specialization, she stopped at the corner lawyer's office and told the receptionist that she needed a new will.

When the lawyer realized how much money the lady had, she charged $250,000 to write a simple will. By now, you know that the job took less than an hour; her hourly rate was pretty good.

Fortunately, the accountant who was reporting the events to me knew enough to challenge the lawyer. He confronted her and told her that he was going to report her to the bar if she didn't refund most of the fee.

Knowing that she had literally robbed a client, the lawyer relented and lowered her fee to $5,000, thus, earning only $5,000 per hour.

Accountants:

Accountants serve a valuable service in our society ... and, as our state and federal tax laws become more and more complex, their services are becoming even more valuable.

Unfortunately, accountants, even Certified Public Accountants (CPA), have very little formal training in estate planning.

A small percentage of them have applied their minds to learning the estate planning process and have become quite expert. But, in the preparation for CPA status, they are not required to learn much about estate planning.

A case in point.

Thinking of how much accountants need good estate planning information, I called the Institute of Accountancy in New York to talk with the man who controls the curriculum for all the courses offered to accountants through this institution. The gentleman was courteous and interested and noted, "We have estate planning courses."

Amazed, I repeated, "You teach no estate planning courses to the accountants?"

"That's right," he said. "We do *not* teach estate planning."

I love to work with accountants. For the most part, they are eager to learn and help their clients save taxes; but I never approach an accountant with the belief that he or she will know much about estate planning.

One of the greatest professional pleasures I have is to get the client, the attorney and the accountant into one room and to outline my plan for the estate plan. With all of these present, I am usually able to communicate both the common-sense and the technical kinds of information.

Bring your accountant to the meeting, but do not expect him to be an expert in estate planning.

Insurance Agents:

While insurance contracts can be very effective estate planning devices, most insurance professionals put too much emphasis on life insurance ... to the detriment of the client.

Many of them come to the problem with a mental approach that says, "Insurance is the answer ... now, tell me the problem."

Repeatedly, people have come to me with a single estate planning device, an insurance policy. They had met with their insurance agent and he had told them that they were facing a large estate tax bill at death ... and had recommended a large life insurance policy.

Most insurance agents do not show people how they can avoid taxes; they just show them how they can buy enough life insurance to pay the taxes.

Wouldn't it be more honest to show them how to avoid the taxes?

Many of them do not know how to avoid taxes.

This came to my attention rather shockingly when I designed the personal estate plan for a 30-year veteran of the life insurance business. Owning his own agency in the Florida Panhandle and being a good businessman, he had amassed an estate of $2 million.

"But," he commented in our meeting, "even though I have sold many life insurance policies over the last 30 years, I did not know that a person could use his lifetime exemption of $600,000 during life. I thought a person had to die to use the $600,000.

"Only when you showed us in the seminar did I learn the $600,000 is usable during life," he concluded.

Using the lifetime exemption during life is a common means of saving estate tax for many estate planning professionals; but this 30-year insurance professional did not know it.

Life insurance people assume that everyone wants to leave everything he has earned to his children. If the client has amassed an estate of $3 million, they assume that he wants his children to have $3 million.

However, that is not always the case.

An Alabama grandfather asked me during an estate planning session, "How much of my $2 million estate do you think I should leave to my granddaughter?"

I replied, "That's not a question I can answer. Only you can determine that."

He agreed. He said, "I think I will leave her $600,000."

Continuing, he noted, "I had nothing when I started out ... and I am not so sure that it is good for people to have too much money. If I left her $600,000, that would be considerably more than I had ... and I think it is enough."

Subsequently, he told me that he planned to leave the balance to charity.

With this approach, $600,000 to granddaughter and the rest to charity, there would be no federal estate tax. Hence, there would be no need to purchase life insurance with which to pay the tax.

Bill Gates, of Microsoft fame, plans a similar approach. Although he is purported to be the richest man in America, with a net worth exceeding $38 billion (with a B), the Time Magazine edition of January 13, 1997 noted that he planned to leave each of his children only $10 million.

Gates plans to leave the rest of his estate to charity.

Be wary of those insurance people who try to sell you too much insurance. There may be better ways to solve your problem.

Journalists:

Reporters, often in need of meeting a deadline, pick up a report from a company and report it with no perspective. Too often, they merely parrot what the company "flack" has prepared for their daily feeding time. Instead of critically reviewing the material, they may just re-phrase it and report it.

A May 5, 1996, story in the Washington Post is a good example. Albert B. Crenshaw, a Post writer copied nearly his entire story from a Merrill Lynch report and said that a survey "covered people over 45." To the uncritical reader, this quote would indicate that the survey covered all people, or a representative group of people, over 45.

A critical review of the story, however, shows that the survey did not claim to be either universal or representative. In fact, the report is worthless as reported.

It appears that Merrill Lynch surveyed some of its *customers* ... and, of course, they are not representative of the American public because most people are not Merrill Lynch customers.

Crenshaw did his readers a disservice by failing to properly identify the population surveyed.

When reading anything, pin down the exact nature of the statistics. For the most part, journalist have little statistical knowledge, consequently providing an incorrect slant to a given datum or to a statistical report.

Crenshaw (and his editors) again demonstrated their sloppiness when he wrote in the special "seniors section" of The Washington Post Health Insert on January 28, 1997, that there is a $600,000 "credit" from estate tax.

As a long-time financial writer, Crenshaw should know the difference in a tax exemption and a tax credit. One doesn't need to be an expert estate planner to know that difference.

There is a $600,000 lifetime exemption from taxation. If a person were to pay tax on that first $600,000, he would pay a tax of $192,800. Because there is no tax on the first $600,000 in an estate, he receives a credit of $192,800.

There is *no* $600,000 credit. There is a $600,000 *exemption* and a $192,800 *credit*.

If there were a $600,000 tax credit, the lifetime exemption from taxation would be about $1.5 million.

If The Washington Post and their financial writer, Crenshaw, want to venture into the field of estate planning, they should do their readers the service of providing accurate information.

Psychological Counselors:

Much of the estate planning advice given to people suffering mental stress is provided by psychological counselors. Generally, neither the counselor nor the counselee is aware that the advice is estate planning advice. The counselor and the counselee are usually concentrating on the psychic pain and its eradication.

Psychological counselors should, to every degree possible, keep their estate planning opinions to themselves.

Professional people can be of great assistance to you in the estate planning process. But *you* must be the captain of your estate planning team. You must learn to ask hard questions, to expect clear answers and to watch out for people who have their own agenda.

Professionals can help.

And they can harm.

Double check everything and educate yourself in every possible way. You and your family must live with the product of the planning process.

FUN QUIZ

CHAPTERS ONE THROUGH NINE

1. T F Most attorneys are paid by the hour.

2. T F Transferring assets to children never creates a taxable event.

3. T F The $600,000 lifetime exemption can be used during life.

4. T F The annual exclusion from taxes is $600,000.

5. T F When children divorce, the judge always returns gifted property back to the parents who gave it.

6. T F Purchasing life insurance saves taxes.

7. T F A tax credit can be claimed only on a Visa card.

8. T F The three secret words of estate planning are "Show me money."

9. T F The Safety Net Trust can benefit grandchildren.

10. T F If you like, you can create a trust to benefit IRS agents.

Test answers are shown on Page 221.

CHAPTER TEN

PROBATE: AVOID IT LIKE THE PLAGUE

In order to make sure that no one stole anything from the decedent or his estate ... and in order to protect the rights of legitimate heirs, all states have a process that consists of a series of events and is summed up in the general term "probate."

When a person who had a will drawn dies, his would-be executor, or some other person, takes that will to the probate court and submits it for probate.

If the judge believes that the presented will is, indeed, the decedent's legitimate last will and testament, he admits that will to probate and appoints an executor or personal representative. Normally, the person appointed is the one nominated in the will.

The judge then gives this person a letter authorizing him to act or to "execute" for the estate of the deceased.

At this point, the Executor has many tasks to perform. He secures all the decedent's property; he may need to appraise it for state or federal tax purposes. He fills out tax forms, pays bills and generally sees to it that the affairs of the decedent are properly wound up and that the assets are passed on to the legitimate heirs.

For this task, the Executor is paid a fee from the estate.

This is time-consuming. While many probates take much longer and, obviously, some require less time, the average probate in America takes one and one-half years to complete.

It is also an expensive process; the average estate is charged six to eight percent of the estate for the entire probate process. Again, some probates cost less; but many cost much more than six to eight percent.

By the way, that is six to eight percent of the *gross* estate. If your estate includes a $100,000 house that has a mortgage balance of $50,000, you and I would think that the probate fee should be figured on the $50,000 sum.

But lawyers' math comes into play here.

The probate establishment has colluded to calculate the fee on the *gross* estate; in this case, on the $100,000 value of the house.

Need I say more about the excessive probate fee process?

Fees are not, to many people, the worst part of probate. It is the invasion of their privacy that they hate the most. Probate is a public process. Neighbors, business competitors, distant relatives and anyone else who is interested may, in most cases, visit the courthouse and read the probate file, including the will.

As a result of the many negative aspects of the probate process, more and more people are choosing estate planning instruments that allow them to avoid the probate process in whole or in part.

Assets in a Living Revocable Trust avoid probate. Moneys in a Pay-on-Death bank account avoid it ... and a piece of real estate left by life estate deed or by joint deed avoids it. Life insurance proceeds paid directly to a named beneficiary avoid the probate plague.

A 20-YEAR PROBATE

At a luncheon with several financial professionals in Frederick, Maryland in May of 1991, I went through the buffet line and, seeing no acquaintances, sat down at a group table where I knew no one.

During the usual introductions, both of the two women beside me indicated they were Certified Public Accountants.

When they learned I was an estate planner, we began to discuss the subject.

One of them noted, "I just closed a probate that has been in process for twenty years."

Somewhat surprised, I said, "Twenty years?"

"Yes," she explained. "One of the beneficiaries died immediately after the decedent and it caused all kinds of problems. My firm has had the probate for many years. Actually, I 'inherited' this probate file after joining the firm five years ago. The total time of probate was twenty years."

Also incredulous, the other CPA chimed in. "That is an extraordinarily long time. My longest probate case lasted just ten years."

Living, as we do, in a "7-Eleven" society where we expect to drive up to a convenience store, go in, purchase our merchandise and get out in just a minute, most of us are not aware that we face a probate system, at some time in our lives, that could take an enormous amount of our precious time.

While the twenty-year probate and the ten-year probate are extraordinary cases, they prove that probate can be a very lengthy process.

PROBATE: NOT SO BAD IN OUR STATE

One of the worst features of probate is the thousands of so-called professionals, all over America, who shout from the roof tops that "probate isn't all that bad."

Attorney William (Bill) Conway practices law in the Washington, DC, area. From time to time, Bill and I get together to discuss estate planning in general and specific cases, in particular.

One day we were talking about probate ... and Bill expressed an interesting series of thoughts.

Bill said, "Every attorney says, 'Probate isn't bad in our state; but in (whatever state is next door) it is a nightmare.'"

I replied that my experience bore out his assertion.

PROBATE: NOT SO BAD IN THIS STATE

In Philadelphia, one of my associates attended a meeting where an attorney spoke and said, "Now, probate isn't so bad here in Pennsylvania; but across the river in New Jersey ... it's bad."

In Maryland, I was working with an attorney and his clients. When the subject of probate came up, he said, "Now, probate isn't so bad here in Maryland; but across the state line in Delaware ... it's bad."

A Virginia lawyer attended one of my seminars in Harrisonburg and told me that she thought that I was too harsh on the probate system because "... probate isn't so bad here in Virginia."

117

She went on to say, "I admit probate is bad over there in West Virginia. But, here in Virginia ... ,it's not so bad."

I was really shocked one day when a Buffalo, New York, counselee told me he planned to allow his estate to go through probate, "Because probate isn't so bad in New York."

Make no mistake about it. Probate is bad.

THE PROBATE ESTABLISHMENT: OUR PRODUCT IS "NOT SO BAD."

If you and I sold refrigerators and our lead advertising line was "Our Refrigerators Aren't So Bad," how many would we sell?

I can see the two of us now, standing on the corner, holding up a sign for passers-by to see:

"Our Refrigerators Aren't So Bad"

Quick, go make the advertising sign. While you are gone, I will open a bank account so we can deposit all the money we will earn. Then we can retire in the lap of luxury.

Yet the probate establishment continues to thrive with this line as their advertising lead.

"Probate isn't so bad in our state."

After years of meditating on this statement, their common lead line, and after all those years of not understanding what they meant, it finally came to me last year.

In a flash, like a bolt out of the blue, I finally comprehended the meaning of ...

"Probate ain't so bad in our state."

They actually mean that
"Probate isn't so bad for
the probate establishment."

Actually, it is quite good for them.

Bad for their clients; but good for them.

The next time someone tells you that, "Probate isn't so bad in our state," ask him this question.

"For whom?"

A 10 PERCENT PROBATE FEE

A community newspaper, <u>The Prince William (VA) Journal</u>, carried this story.

An attorney had charged a one hundred thousand dollar ($100,000) probate fee when his only duty, as executor, was to change the deed on a tract of land from the decedent to her daughters. The land value was about one million dollars.

His fee amounted to ten percent of the estate.

Because changing a deed is done in a matter of minutes, usually by an attorney's clerical staff, the family contended that the $100,000 fee was excessive.

In his reply to the family's complaint, the attorney admitted that Virginia law specifies that five percent is a reasonable fee when the estate is not difficult to probate. "But," he added, "when told that the five percent fee is normal, my client specifically requested that I charge a ten percent fee."

Now, pardon me for a moment while I try to understand this quixotic statement. Am I understanding it correctly?

He advised her that the fee was normally *five* percent.

But she asked him to charge *ten* percent.

Anybody want to buy a bridge?

ANOTHER 10 PERCENT PROBATE FEE: THIS TIME BY THE GOVERNOR

When a couple came in for estate planning in Baltimore, they told me of their experience in probating their neighbor's estate.

"We really got all the work done," reported the man. "But we thought it might be a good idea to get an attorney to approve of what we had done before we submitted the file to the probate court.

"The only lawyer we knew was a local city councilman; we asked him how much he would charge to look over the file.

"The lawyer said that he would charge ten percent of the estate's value. Although I thought that was awfully high, I knew no other attorneys; so I agreed to the fee."

Then he emphasized, "That price seemed strange to me; but I felt helpless because I just didn't know any other attorneys."

119

Concluding, he said, "Just as he stated, the attorney charged the estate a ten-percent fee when it was all said and done."

Relaxing in my hotel room that evening, I went over the days events in my mind and thought about the story the man had told me. It seemed incredible. A ten-percent fee for doing no more than the man described? Could he have been making up such a story? Could he have been mistaken? Did he have a political motive?

The next day, thinking that the man might have been mistaken or that he might have been guilty of slander, I decided to check up on the story. Having a break in my work at mid-day, I drove down to the Baltimore City Court House to look up the file of the decedent.

Sure enough, the attorney had charged a fee equal to ten percent of the estate's value. There it was in black and white. A ten-percent fee.

To add insult to injury, the attorney had, apparently, asked two other attorneys to sign affidavits stating that the fee was reasonable for the work done. The affidavits were in the file.

Just as the man had said, the attorney was City Councilman William Donald Shaeffer, who later became Mayor of the city and, eventually, Governor of Maryland.

Amazed and astounded, I gazed at the file and asked myself the question, "Even the Governor ... ?"

WHEN CHARITY WAS ROBBED OF $90,000 BY PROBATE

Visiting a non-profit retirement home in Southern Pennsylvania, I was told this story by the Director of Development.

"A lady in our community died and left an estate of $900,000 entirely to charity. Half was to go to our cause and half to another local charity.

"The estate consisted of one item, a bank account where the $900,000 was deposited.

"Not long after the death, her attorney called me and said that he was taking a fee of $45,000 for probating the estate and that he was going to award a similar amount to the lady's niece for her role as executor. He also asked me to sign a letter saying that I agreed that these fees were reasonable.

120

"I refused to sign the letter. But," he went on, "that did not deter the lawyer. He proceeded to take $90,000 out of the estate for legal and executor fees. All that for his work of moving the money from one bank account to another."

While we would not argue that the lawyer and the executor should have a reasonable compensation for their work, this fee was outrageous and was charged only because the antiquated laws of the state allowed it.

A WILL PROBATED AT THE BRIDGE CLUB

In Virginia's Shenandoah Valley, an 87-year-old lady came in for personal estate planning. She was mentally and physically active and looked fifteen years younger than she admitted.

She wanted to make some revisions in her estate plan.

"I lived most of my life in Cleveland, Ohio," she began. "My first husband and I had a good life there and, to this day, I love the city of Cleveland."

"When I was in my sixties, my dear husband died," she said.

"Some time later, at a college reunion in Massachusetts, I met one of my gentlemen friends from college days. His wife had died the year before.

"Soon, we began to write to one another ... and he came up from Virginia to visit me several times. We became close friends and, after several visits, we decided to marry. I moved here to Virginia and we married when I was 70.

"We had a good marriage for our ten years together before he died. He was a wonderful man and I am pleased and proud that I moved here and that we had such a wonderful life together.

"But, after he died, I was shocked to learn that one of my bridge club members went down to the county court house and reviewed my husband's estate. She brought all the details back to the bridge club. For two years, my husband's financial affairs were the main subject of gossip at the bridge club."

Concluding her story, she said, "My husband's estate was probated at the local bridge club."

As epilogue, she pointedly stated, "Mr. Recer, tell everybody who attends your seminars to avoid probate. I don't wish the embarrassment of a bridge-club probate on anyone."

"GOING THROUGH HELL WITH PROBATE"

In the midst of presenting a seminar at the Greater Baltimore Medical Center, I was somewhat surprised when a woman stood up in the rear of the audience and asked to speak.

I learned long ago that spontaneity is sometimes the spice of a good public meeting, so I gave her the floor.

She said, "I'm going through hell with my parents' probate.

"My whole family is from Pennsylvania. I moved down here to Baltimore many years ago; but Father and Mother continued to live in Pennsylvania. Father died seven years ago ... and, as Executrix, I began the probate process. Before I could get Father's estate probated, Mother died.

"Consequently, I then started probating Mother's estate. For seven years I have been constantly traveling back and forth to Pennsylvania and working on the two probates.

"The worst thing," she said, "is that the attorney won't even let me see the will."

A gasp went through the crowd.

"That's right," she said, "she won't even let me see the will."

I assured her that, as Executrix, she had every right to see and to review all the relevant papers.

I suggested she talk with me after the seminar when I could give her situation additional personal attention.

In our post-seminar session, the President of the hospital foundation and I tried to help her; and we succeeded to some degree. Nothing we could do or say could compensate her for the time, effort, frustration and misery that she had gone through for seven long years of probate.

So, when some member of the probate establishment tells you that "Probate isn't so bad here in our state," remember the story of the woman who told the Baltimore crowd that she had been through Hell with her parents' probates.

PROBATE: "CHEAP AND EASY IN OUR STATE"

When I conducted the personal estate planning sessions following the Basic Estate Seminar for the Armed Services YMCA in El Paso, I asked the "Y" personnel if they could provide me a list of local attorneys so I could give the names to my counselees.

The Director, Art Sears, replied, "I don't know any estate planning attorneys. Will you help us locate some?"

I looked in the yellow pages and found a listing of attorneys who are 'Board Certified in Estate Planning and Probate' by the Texas Board of Legal Specialization.

Among those listed, I recognized the name of a classmate from undergraduate college days.

Wondering if it really could be the same person, I called to find out. Sure enough, it was the classmate. We renewed our acquaintance ... and I told him the purpose of my call.

He graciously offered to come over to the hotel, pick me up, take me to dinner and provide any assistance I needed.

We stopped at his office where he showed me his personally programmed estate planning computer program and other indicators of his work in the field. He claimed to be doing 600 probates per year.

I asked if he ever did any living revocable trusts (to avoid probate) and he replied:

"No need to. Texas probate is so quick, easy, simple and economical that there is little need for living trusts."

He then proceeded to tell me that, in Texas, you can self-administer the probate. Therefore, you do not need to get the judge's permission all along the way.

His defense of the Texas probate system was lengthy, emphatic and detailed.

When we parted, I thought about his very strong belief in the Texas probate system and I said to myself, "That's wonderful. I am so glad to know that there is a state where probate is no problem. When I present the seminar later this week, I may just 'soft pedal' the living trust because, according to my fellow alumnus, 'Probate is so simple here that there is little need to avoid it.'"

Arriving early for my seminar presentation on Saturday morning, I waited while the crowd gathered.

A copy of the day's El Paso Herald-Post had been delivered to the desk near where I was sitting, so I picked up the newspaper and glanced at it.

Page one of the April 6, 1991, edition carried the following story:

"Commissioner Charles Hooten had a good idea about how to use a court master to clean up the probate mess in the five county Courts-At-Law.

"He tried to boost the notion to pay a court master around $65,000 per year to do the job rather than to load up taxpayers with a sixth county Court-At-Law judge, at $86,000 plus.

"But Hooten was out voted in what resulted in an academic exercise anyway because commissioners don't have enough new revenues for a sixth judge anyway.

"Hooten, however, thinks he might have another idea for how to get cobwebs off the probate piles judges are so squeamish about.

"He says there's a law requiring judges to formally perform reviews on their stashes of probate cases, and Hooten wants to find out which judges are doing their duties.

"Probate matters have been sensitive since last year when one of the local brethren was indicted and de-benched in a scheme where *several estates* under his judicial care *were ripped off*."

Shocked that the probate system was so corrupt in this area of Texas ... and that my alumnus had failed to tell me of the saga that had been brewing for some time, I resolved to show the seminar audience a better way; the living revocable trust way of avoiding probate.

I revised my plans about soft-pedaling the LRT and gave the people my usual strong dose of anti-probate medicine.

Probate can be a horrendous experience in any state. If your estate is, in any way, complicated, you should consider some form of probate avoidance.

A NINE-YEAR PROBATE
In Charleston, South Carolina, Mr. Howard D. Peckenpaugh, of the College of Charleston, told me of a new company designed to help

people avoid probate. It was founded by a woman, Ellie Alpert, whose husband's estate took over ten years to probate.

About three years into the terribly frustrating probate experience, she was thinking, "There must be a better way." She soon learned that there is a better way, the Living Revocable Trust.

Amazed that there was, indeed, such an easy way to avoid the whole probate system, she determined to learn all about this mechanism. After considerable work and research, she had become an expert on the subject; soon, she became a vociferous advocate for this means of probate avoidance.

Tongue in cheek, she says, "I was stopping people on the street to tell them about it."

Now, she and her employees at Trust Associates hold seminars to inform the public about the evils of probate and about the living trust solution.

Ellie is a wonderful example of someone who doggedly refused to let the system beat her. Even though the probate establishment cost her a horrific price in time, money and frustration, she has saved many others a similar fate by showing them how to beat the system.

A FIFTY-THOUSAND-DOLLAR PROBATE

Showing me a picture of a perfectly restored Chesapeake Bay mansion, a Southern Maryland woman told me that she and her husband had purchased the property in run-down condition twenty-five years earlier for eighteen thousand dollars.

"We put eight hundred thousand dollars and twenty years of elbow grease into this house," she explained.

"But my husband died two years ago ..., and his death caused me to lose interest in the house. Now, I am trying to sell it for what the realtors tell me it is worth, one and a half million dollars."

She continued, "However, I can't sell it until the probate is finished.

"When we purchased the property, my husband and I were advised to take title to the house 'tenants in common' and we followed that advice. When he died, his 'tenants in common' share went into probate where the probate establishment has kept it two years.

"I am so angry at everybody involved in this probate that I can't sleep at night and I think about it every living minute. So far, I have spent forty-five thousand dollars to clear up the title. The lawyer tells me that he can finish next week if I bring in an additional $6,000.

"Even though I hate to spend any more money, I am going to cash in some stock and take the money down there to his office just to get this terrible probate out of my hair. Then, I hope to get on with my life."

She summarized, "Dr. Recer, I hope you will tell everybody, everywhere you go, that they should do everything possible to avoid probate."

I was so horrified by her story ... and so impressed by the depth of her anger ... that I wanted to be sure that someone else would be there to help her after I left town. I walked down the hall to my host's office and asked Graham Lee to come meet the lady and to hear her story.

He was just as shocked and amazed as I was.

A NINETEEN PERCENT PROBATE FEE

A friend of mine, a banker in Washington, DC, told me this story.

When a local couple was killed in an auto crash, the only asset in their estate was their $90,000 town house. Their only heir was their son, a twenty-five-year-old who was learning-disabled and who was marginally employed.

Some weeks after the death, the probate lawyer approached the bank and said that he needed a loan of $20,000 on the house. He indicated that the young man would sign the note and that the house would stand as collateral.

My friend (who prefers to remain anonymous) and other bank executives were involved in the loan-approval process.

Observing the young man's employment status and credit record, my friend argued against making the loan. She said to her colleagues, "Where will this young man get the money to pay the $200-per-month loan payment?"

But she was out-voted and the bank made the loan.

When it came time for the loan settlement, my friend reviewed the closing statement and was outraged. She saw that the probate attorney was to be paid $17,000 of the $20,000 directly out of the loan proceeds.

The learning disabled young man walked away with only $3,000 and the burden of making the $200 payments.

But he never paid a dime.

Getting into trouble with the law, he ended up in jail; and, of course, made no payments.

To protect its stockholders and depositors, the bank foreclosed on the house.

All the young man got out of the deal was the $3,000, which he rapidly spent.

The probate lawyer, however, got paid in full. He made $17,000 on a $90,000 estate. His fee amounted to nineteen percent of the deceased couple's lifetime savings, their house.

The lawyer had arranged the loan for one reason and one reason only ... to be sure that he got his money.

The bottom line is that probate is, at best, a gamble. It may take six months ... or it may take twenty years.

It may cost three percent ... or it may cost fifteen percent.

It may not reveal any sensitive private information ... or it may open the family's business to the wrong people.

Avoid probate like the plague.

FUN QUIZ

CHAPTERS ONE THROUGH TEN

1. T F   Probate is a public process.

2. T F   Probate can last for years.

3. T F   Those who advocate the probate process have as their best advertisement that "it isn't so bad."

4. T F   Probate is always completed in 30 days time.

5. T F   Assets in a Living Revocable Trust avoid probate.

6. T F   Avoiding probate does not automatically mean that one avoids estate tax.

7. T F   Probate "ain't so bad" in the state of Delusion.

8. T F   Both the lawyer and the executor may claim a fee.

9. T F   Assets transferred to a Safety Net Trust during life do not go through probate.

10. T F   Proceeds of a life insurance policy, payable to a named beneficiary, do not go through probate.

Test answers are shown on Page 222.

CHAPTER ELEVEN

HUMAN VALUES:
THE KEYSTONE OF ESTATE PLANNING

One couple came to me for estate planning and said they had been disappointed and put off by their lawyer's approach to estate planning. They told me that they had gone to the lawyer and briefly asked his estate planning advice.

The lawyer quickly cracked,
"Just tell me how much you've got ...
and I will plan your estate."

To him, estate planning was, evidently, nothing more than a mathematical equation. This "number-cruncher" approach to estate planning ignores all the human values that rightfully should guide the planning process.

Human values evidently have no place in his planning technique; by his way of thinking, estate planning can be performed by an automaton.

Fortunately, the couple who came to see me and on whom he tried his technique did not buy it. They were able to see through this shallow manner of thinking. They were courageous enough to go elsewhere for their help. These people were wise enough to know that estate planning is more than a financial formula. They understood that their estate plan could be an expression of their values.

Estate planning is "The Art and Science of Planning for Estate Distribution."

More than the scientific application of mathematical formulae, ... and more than the crafty application of social techniques, estate planning is both a science and an art.

EXPRESSING INDIVIDUALITY

Everywhere we look in American society today, people are striving to express their specific and individual identity. Via their clothing choices, bodily adornments, musical expressions ... and in many other ways, multitudes of people are trying to show exactly how they stand out from the herd. People want to be recognized as distinct individuals.

Certainly, they have every right to express their individuality in any legal and ethical manner they may choose.

However, when it comes to planning their estate, ninety-five percent of them allow their advisor to shove a form-book will down their throat. As if dispensing widgets from the factory, many advisors want their clients to take a cookie-cutter will off the shelf, sign it and ask as few questions as possible.

Consequently, the same people who strive so mightily to express their individuality in life ... give little thought to the multitude of ways they can more indelibly leave their unique mark when they pass from this life.

Many people are simply unaware of the variety of ways they can express themselves via a last statement of their individuality. Of that ignorance, all of us in the estate planning profession bear some responsibility.

There is, however, that other small percentage of people who recognize the unique opportunity they have to express themselves in an estate plan. For the most part, these people have used their estate plan as a means of achieving worthy causes.

In my years of conducting personal estate plans, I have come across several people who had given this matter considerable thought and who, therefore, were able to stamp their permanent imprint in a unique manner.

Here are a few of those people:

TWO MILLION DOLLARS TO VIRGINIA TECH

Conducting personal estate plans one day in Arlington, Virginia, I had the pleasure of meeting an 82-year-old stockbroker who felt very warmly toward his alma mater, Virginia Tech. Having graduated from the college at Blacksburg nearly sixty years earlier, he continued to carry the institution in his heart.

Having no children, he and his wife decided to provide for the University in their estate plan. Because of his profession, he narrowed the plan down to a specific cause.

"College kids get absolutely no training in all the elements of financial planning," he said.

"I graduated as an engineer, and for some time, thought I would follow that profession. But, along the way, I became exposed to Wall Street and became enamored with it. I have spent most of my life since college days as a stockbroker. I am quite pleased that I have been able to help so many people succeed with their investments.

"In addition," he continued, "my wife and I have amassed an estate of over $2 million. With no children, we had to decide what to do with it when we are gone."

He said, "I went down to the University to visit the Dean of the College of Business. I told him I wanted to leave all $2 million of our estate to the school to found a program that would ensure that every student had some opportunity to learn the elements of financial planning.

"Of course, the Dean was happy to learn of my intent. In fact, he was so happy that he shook my hand three times before I left his office."

I was amused at the story of the "three-hand-shake" Dean, so, with a smile, I congratulated the octogenarian.

"You and your wife are to be commended for your vision. It sounds to me as though you have designed a plan that carries on the values you have been practicing for over half a century.

"Your estate will continue helping people manage their money for many years after you are gone."

"That's exactly what we have tried to do," he said.

Sensing that he might be a better financial planner than an estate planner ... and knowing from his presence at my seminar and in my personal estate planning session, that he would welcome any suggestions I might make, I asked, "Exactly how are you planning to make this transfer to the college?"

"My lawyer told me to do it in a will; so that's what we have done," he replied.

"Have you ever considered a charitable trust?" I asked.

"Of course, I have heard about them; but I don't know much about them because I have just never thought about trusts very much."

I explained that he and his wife could create a charitable remainder trust and begin making some transfers to it during life. They would receive income from the trust for their lives. Each year they transferred stock or money to the trust, they would earn an income tax deduction.

Each income tax deduction would, in essence, augment his estate. With a smaller portion of his income going for taxes each year, he would be keeping more money and enlarging his estate.

He brightened. "We could leave even more to the college, couldn't we?"

"You catch on quickly," I said.

He was genuinely delighted to have found a way to give more money to his college.

I had a warm feeling in my heart at the end of our meeting. For two reasons. The couple had found their way of expressing themselves via the estate plan ... and that felt good.

In addition, I was able to show the gentleman a way to enhance and improve an already-excellent plan. That felt good, too.

THE CHILDREN WILL HAVE SOMETHING IN COMMON

In Martinsville, Virginia, I met with a couple who had an estate of eight million dollars. Community minded and wanting to do good things for their charities and for their family, they were eager to learn and easy to work with. I had the pleasure of helping them create an effective and rather unique estate plan.

Among the planning elements I suggested was the use of a charitable remainder trust in a very special way.

Having already explained to them that they could create the trust during life and that the two of them could receive income from it, I suggested an eventual transfer of assets to the trust in the amount of about three million dollars.

Depending on the exact way in which these transfers were made, the tax savings could be about two million dollars. The estate tax savings would be about $1.5 million. If some of the gifts were made during life, the couple would also save an enormous amount of income tax.

"We've paid enough taxes," the man said. "I like the idea of saving both income tax and estate tax."

I told them of another feature I thought they would like. "If you chose to design the charitable trust in a certain way, you could make it convert to a family foundation after both of you are gone. Your money could continue to benefit your community for many years.

"Your children could then become the trustees of the trust and could work together to carry out your charitable intent."

The woman showed intense interest.

I continued, "For example, if the two of you decided that the charitable purpose of your family foundation was, 'To conduct any worthy charitable enterprise in the area around Martinsville, Virginia,' your children, as trustees of the foundation, would, annually, make decisions as to which particular local charitable causes they would benefit.

"They would give away an amount equal to at least five percent of the foundation's assets each year."

Turning to her husband, the woman said, 'I really like this plan. This would give the kids something in common. It would give them something they could all work on together ... and I think it would help them stay together. It would be a means of keeping the family on the same charitable track that we have enjoyed so much."

The couple adopted the plan, a means of caring for their charities and of keeping their family focused on a common goal.

A SCHOLARSHIP FOR NURSING STUDENTS

Meeting with my estate planning counselees in a conference room just down the hall from the nursing school at The Memorial Hospital at Easton, Maryland, I had no idea that the next person would want to provide a scholarship for that very nursing school.

Toward the end of my meeting with the woman, she said, "Even though I haven't practiced nursing in many years, I still consider it my primary profession and I have a warm place in my heart for young people who choose to enter the profession."

Then she asked, "Could I set up a scholarship for nurses right here in the nursing school?"

I assured her that I thought it was possible ... and then I went down the hall to the office of the hospital's chief development official and asked him to help explain the options to the lady.

During their conversation, she told him of her days in school and of the great satisfaction she received from practicing nursing. "I still miss it," she confessed. "Now that I have a substantial estate of my own, I would like to help some young people get their start in the profession."

When we finished, she assured us that she was going to instruct her lawyer to help her set up a scholarship program via her living revocable trust. With a spring in her step, she left the building.

Her deep-seated joy from her nursing years became the engine of her estate planning enterprise.

MY LATE DAUGHTER, THE PILOT

Presenting an estate planning seminar in behalf of Dowling College which has an outstanding transportation program that includes a series of aircraft-related courses and programs, I was approached at the seminar break by a woman who asked if she could talk with me after the seminar.

When we sat down to talk, she said, "My daughter was a pilot and was killed three years ago in an airplane crash.

"The probate problem has been horrendous because she owned property in three states, Massachusetts, New Jersey and New York. We are just about through with all the probate and I want to set up a scholarship in her name here at Dowling."

"How can I help?" I asked.

"My sister and I want to set it up now ... and then make some gifts to it through our estates. Can we do that?"

I assured her that such a plan was possible and that I would talk with the college officials and get back to her.

It was a simple operation.

Here is just one more example of a family member using an estate to further the memory of a loved one.

In this case, three different estates would eventually come into play and would honor the life and work of the daughter who loved aviation so much and who, unfortunately, lost her life in the pursuit of her treasured profession.

I DON'T WANT TO GIVE MY GRANDKIDS TOO MUCH.

One of the greatest college presidents in America is Dr. Jim Taylor of Cumberland Colleges in Williamsburg, Kentucky. One day I got a call from Jim asking me to meet with one of his donors to help plan his estate.

Arrangements were made and, in a few days, I was facing the man in the Buckhead Club high above that elegant part of Atlanta known by the same name.

A successful sales executive, the donor had began investing in real estate many years before and ... during the conversation, told me of several tracts of valuable real estate that he owned.

At one point, he said, "Come over here by the window and I'll show you one of my properties."

I walked to the window and he pointed south down the highway known locally as "The 400." He said, "See where that shopping center is?"

I nodded.

"I own the tract of land on the 400 just beyond the shopping center."

He told me he started out in business at age 14 by repairing bicycles ... and soon realized the value of enterprise, capitalism and investing.

It was an interesting and inspiring story.

He never summarized his estate; so I didn't know exactly how much it was worth. Trying to follow my assigned mission of helping this gentleman plan his estate, I finally said, "It sounds to me like you have an estate of about $10 million."

"More like 20," he replied.

Digesting that bit of information, I proceeded to show him some means of estate planning.

Pulling out a series of paper graphics, I showed him some of the estate planning devices that we use in our practice. When I came to the page that describes trusts for children or grandchildren, he stopped me.

"I really like that trust for the grandchildren," he said. " I like what you say about being able to limit how much each of them can receive each year."

He added, "I don't think it is a good idea to give kids too much money."

Then he explained how he was helping his granddaughter with her college finances and indicated he was happy to help to a limited degree. He emphasized, however, his strong belief that young people should learn to be resourceful and independent and they should respect the value of a dollar.

He was, in this sense, definitely from the old school.

While this man could give his heirs any amount of money he chose, he preferred to use a trust that would limit their stream of income. His personal value system was built on a belief that young people do better if they are not given too much; if they are encouraged to use their own resources.

By using some rather standard estate planning devices, he was able to translate his values into an estate plan.

ONE-THIRD TO THIS ORGANIZATION BECAUSE IT IS THE ONE WHO HELPED US UNDERSTAND ESTATE PLANNING

Like most Americans, I remember what I was doing on certain days that have historical significance.

As a five-year-old boy,
asking my parents,
"What does 'war' mean?"
on December 7, 1941.

As a fourteen-year-old paper route delivery boy,
opening my papers at 3:30 a.m.
to see the headline
"North Koreans cross the 38th parallel."

As a 27-year-old teacher,
hearing the school speaker system tell us
The President was dead
on November 22, 1963.

And, I remember what I was doing on the day of the Challenger disaster.

On that morning, January 28, 1986, I was conducting personal estate planning sessions in a suite at the Hyatt Hotel in Richmond, Virginia.

To keep tabs on the anticipated space shot while sharing the estate planning concepts with the people who were coming in for estate planning conferences, I kept the television turned on and muted. Periodically, while counseling the people, I would watch the Challenger saga out of the corner of my eye.

A few days earlier, I had conducted an estate planning seminar in behalf of a cancer organization at the Marriott Hotel in downtown Richmond. Because most of the people who attended the seminar were cancer donors, several of those who asked for a personal estate planning session wanted to include the cause of cancer in their estate plans.

One couple came in and told me that they had no children.

"Each of us has one sister," the man reported. "We want one-third of our estate to go to each of them."

"Okay, I can help you with that," I said. "What about the other third?"

"We want that to go to charities," he replied. "One-third of it to our church, one-third to the American Heart Association and one-third to this organization because they offered us the opportunity to understand this estate planning routine."

Just about the time that he told me of the "thirds," I noticed the television screen and the strange-looking cloud that the Challenger left.

"I think something went wrong," I said.

We turned up the volume to find that the Challenger crew had perished.

And that's why I remember so vividly the couple who had decided so carefully where their values lay and how they wanted their estate divided.

Loving their sisters, they provided for them. Then they cared for some specific charitable causes. Two of those causes were served because they meant a lot to the people. The cancer cause benefited because the people appreciated our helping them to understand the entire process.

Their estate plan was certainly a reflection of their values. It was, in no way, a cookie-cutter plan.

CAN I GIVE MY KIDS A TRIP TO EUROPE EVERY SUMMER?

As an advocate of trusts in estate planning, I often explain to people that they can create a trust for their children and allow that trust to pay benefits to the children in any way they want.

We often use the Safety Net Trust to pay out three benefits to a generation at one time. These are:

1. All income.

2. Five percent if they want it.

3. Anything else for their Health, Education, Maintenance and Support if they need it.

The Safety Net Trust can be designed to provide any other benefit that a person wants.

When I described this trust to one woman, she replied, "I like to give my kids a trip to Europe every summer. Can I put in the trust 'trip to Europe every summer?'"

I assured her she could and that her trustee would be required to carry out her instructions.

With that bit of information, she indicated she wanted such a trust because it would help her carry out her values. In this case, a trip to Europe every summer.

138

I DON'T WANT HER PEOPLE TO GET MY MONEY

Working with Rusty Brink of the Fletcher-Allen Health Foundation in Burlington, Vermont, I was able to help one woman to be sure her assets did not go to her daughter-in-law's family.

She told us that she was sixty years of age and that three major events had happened in the past few years.

"I got divorced. I remarried. And my father died.

"With what I had ... and with what daddy left me, I've got about a million dollars," she reported. "And, my new husband has plenty of money."

She paused and added, "We've decided that he will give his money to his family and I will give my money to my family. We have no difference of opinion on that score. We are of one mind.

"Here's my family." She slid some notes across the table toward me.

"Son number one ... and son number two.

"Son number one is married ... and has two kids.

"Son number two is married ... and has muscular dystrophy."

Then she said something extremely rare in my experience.

She said, "I love both my daughters-in-law. Both of them are just like daughters to me. I feel so lucky that I have good ones and I want to provide for them in my estate plan.

"But," she continued while pointing to the name of the daughter-in-law who was married to her critically ill son,

"I don't like her people."

"I don't want her people to get any of my money."

She told us she wanted to help this son and his wife buy a house.

I showed her how to give the son a life estate in the house and how to, subsequently, give the daughter-in-law a life estate.

We call this approach "the consecutive life estate deed" plan.

I said, "By creating a Safety Net Trust for benefit of your grandchildren and by making it the remainderman of the life estate deed, you can be assured that the daughter-in-law's people will not benefit from your estate. They will not get your money."

She readily understood the life estate deed and she adopted the plan.

It fulfilled her values of:
1. Caring for son.
2. Caring for daughter-in-law.
3. Keeping her money from "her people."

WE WANT TO CARE FOR THE SURVIVING WIFE OF OUR MURDERED SON

On January 25, 1993, a young man and his wife, both employed by the CIA, were sitting in their car in the left-turn lane waiting for the green light when a terrorist walked along beside several cars shooting people as they sat helplessly inside their automobiles. The young man, sitting behind the wheel of his car, was fatally wounded.

Most of us remember all to well this terrible senseless attack on the Virginia commuters driving along Route 123 and turning into the Central Intelligence Agency headquarters.

About two years after the incident, I did the estate plan for a Pennsylvania couple whose son was one of the murder victims: the young man.

The couple expressed their desire to include their widowed daughter-in-law in their estate plan because they knew that the incident had taken a terrible toll on her body and soul. They wanted to be sure they did everything possible to help her.

I felt privileged to be of assistance to the elder couple and to feel I had some small part in assuring the daughter-in-law's financial future.

This was definitely a value-driven estate plan.

YOUR VALUES ARE IMPORTANT

Just as the people of whom I have written drove their estate plan by their values, so should you. Your plan can and should be an internally driven one. It should be far more than a financial formula. Don't allow yourself to drive your plan by the mere external mechanism of the tax law. Certainly, we all want to avoid taxes when possible; but your values are more important than the tax law.

140

Your appreciation for certain people, arts, causes, beliefs, folkways, etc. is the place to start. If you have assigned great weight to certain values in your life, you should, in some form or another, reflect those qualities in your plan.

Your plan should be uniquely you. It is not a widget. In no case should it be produced like it came off the factory line. Your plan should be a personal expression, reduced to writing, of who you are and of the values you want your life to perpetuate.

Do not, under any circumstances, allow any one to reduce you and your estate plan to a mathematical formula.

Stay away from lawyers...or anyone else who says,

"Just tell me how much you've got...
and I will plan your estate."

YOUR ESTATE PLAN QUIZ

Instead of a true-false set of items, I am here offering you a place to stamp your person on your estate plan.

Either on this page, or on a separate sheet, take a few moments and respond to these queries.

1. On whose life do you want your life to have made some impact? List the top three to five people.

2. What educational causes have you favored in your life?

3. Which of the arts has your life espoused, or which one would you, had circumstances been different, have liked your life to have impacted?

4. Is there a religious or philosophical cause that you have embraced and that you would like to benefit?

5. Is there someone you specifically want to disinherit?

6. Given the answers to the questions above, how would you like your estate plan to impact each item?

142

CHAPTER TWELVE

THE ELEMENTS OF ESTATE PLANNING

To master the discipline of your estate plan, you must learn a few of the building blocks, a few of the elements that a person can use in an estate plan. You will not need every one of these elements; but you need to understand them so that you can decide which ones you want to tell your estate planning attorney to use.

Following is a list of the basic elements of estate planning. We will discuss each one in a page or two. In addition, we will indicate which ones are generally needed by specific kinds of people.

1. LAST WILL AND TESTAMENT
2. LIVING REVOCABLE TRUST
3. BYPASS TRUST
4. QTIP TRUST
5. SPENDTHRIFT TRUST
6. CHARITABLE REMAINDER TRUST
7. LIFE INSURANCE
8. LIFE INSURANCE TRUST
9. PERSONAL RESIDENCE TRUST (GRIT)
10. THE LIFE ESTATE DEED
11. POWER OF ATTORNEY
12. YOUR RETIREMENT PLAN
13. FAMILY LIMITED PARTNERSHIP
14. "PAY-ON-DEATH" BANK ACCOUNT
15. CRUMMEY TRUST
16. SAFETY NET TRUST

LAST WILL AND TESTAMENT
1. Who needs it?

Every adult should have an up-to-date will.

2. What does it do?

It passes any asset that is not governed by other estate planning devices.

Only 27% of Americans have a will when they die; however, most people should have a will. The will passes any asset that the person owns outright ... that he owns in his own name. It does not pass assets that are owned jointly in a living trust or in some other ways.

While many states allow a person to write his or her own will out in longhand, it is best to have a will drawn by a lawyer licensed to practice law in your state of residence. Each state's laws are slightly different and a local lawyer is most apt to be conversant with those differences.

In most states, you can leave your assets to anyone you please; however, some states allow a widow to claim a part of the estate through a legal procedure called "The Widow's Election." Some states give preferential treatment to your descendants.

State laws differ on the question of naming disinherited heirs in your will. Be sure you know your state law if you decide to disinherit any natural heir.

Be careful that you do not libel anyone by making a disparaging statement such as, "I leave my wish for a life full of heartache to my no-good son-in-law who cheated on my daughter and starved my grandchildren." Such a statement is an invitation to a lawsuit against your estate.

Generally, you want to provide burial or cremation instructions in another instrument; not in the will. The will may not be found and read until after the funeral.

You are not required to record your will at the county courthouse when you have it prepared. It is generally recorded there when it is admitted to probate at your death. However, if you so desire, you can record it prior to death. Some people like to record such documents in order to be sure they are not lost.

Your will does not take effect until your death. You may change it or re-write it at any time that you have a sound mind. If you re-do your will, destroy the old one to avoid confusion.

If you want to add a sentence or two to your will, do so under the supervision of your attorney. He or she will create a formal codicil, or amendment, to your will. Do not write on your typed will or make any notation of any kind on any page except as directed by your attorney in his presence.

THE LIVING REVOCABLE TRUST

1. Who needs it?

Any person who wants to avoid probate.

2. What does it do?

It delivers all its assets directly to the persons, trusts or causes named by its creator (trustor) without the need for probate.

Any trust that becomes effective during your life is a living trust. Such a trust that contains words like the following is a revocable trust.

"I reserve the right at any time to revoke this trust
in whole or in part."

The primary purpose of the Living Revocable Trust (LRT) is to avoid probate. The LRT, in and of itself, does not save taxes. However, it is often used in more sophisticated estate plans, and, along with a Bypass Trust, does save taxes.

A living trust has three primary offices. They are:

1. Trustor
2. Trustee
3. Beneficiary

In most states, one person (you) can fill all three offices.

In addition to these three, you will want a Standby Trustee and a Standby Beneficiary. The Standby, or contingent, Trustee takes over in case of your death or disability. The Standby, or backup, Beneficiary generally does not benefit until the end of your life.

A bank or stockbrokerage trust department is the best Standby Trustee. Either a person, a trust or an institution can be the Standby Beneficiary.

To make an LRT effective, you must fund it. You must put assets into it. Unfortunately, many people think they have an effective LRT; but have never transferred any assets to the trust. Therefore, they have an empty trust ... a mere piece of paper.

People who want to avoid the time, expense and publicity of probate will want an LRT.

THE BYPASS TRUST

1. Who needs it?

Married people who will have a taxable estate by the time the first one dies.

2. What does it do?

It can save over $200,000 from federal estate tax.

The Bypass Trust is used by married people to guarantee that the two lifetime exemptions are properly used. Under current law, it can save as much as $235,000 in federal estate taxes.

The Bypass Trust is not created when you draw up your estate plan. Rather, it is authorized. In your will or in your living trust, you authorize your executor or trustee to create the Bypass Trust at your death. In addition, you may specify certain criteria regarding your Bypass Trust.

Each spouse will need to authorize the Bypass Trust in his or her will or Living Revocable Trust (LRT).

Your LRT might say words to this effect, "If I am the first to die, pay all the tax that will ever be due on my estate." If your half of the estate is $600,000 or less, there will be no tax due. You will have paid "all that is due" and the Bypass Trust can never be taxed again.

The Bypass Trust is designed to benefit the spouse for his or her life. It can be designed to give the spouse.

    1. All income.

    2. Five percent or five thousand (whichever is greater) annually.

    3. Anything needed for the spouse's Health, Education, Maintenance and Support.

At the end of the second spouse's life, the Bypass assets can go to the persons or trusts that were originally named by the first spouse to die.

The beauty of the Bypass Trust is that it can benefit both spouse (as life beneficiary) and other persons or causes (as the ultimate beneficiary). One does not need to choose between spouse and others. Both can receive appropriate benefits.

THE QTIP TRUST
1. Who needs it?

Married people who will have a taxable estate at the death of the first one.

2. What does it do?

The QTIP Trust provides income and other benefits to a surviving spouse ... and, subsequently, passes assets to other people, causes or trusts.

The QTIP Trust is used by married people to guarantee that the first decedent's assets benefit the spouse for his or her life ... and then to guarantee that the first decedent's people or causes receive benefits.

It is generally used in conjunction with a Bypass Trust and it receives the portion of the first decedent's estate that exceeds the exempted amount. The $600,000 amount that is exempt from estate tax goes into the Bypass Trust ... and the remainder goes into the QTIP Trust.

The QTIP Trust is not created when you draw up your estate plan. Rather, it is authorized. In your will or in your Living Revocable Trust (LRT), you authorize your executor or trustee to create the QTIP Trust at your death. In that authorization, you may say how you want the trust designed.

Each spouse will need to authorize the QTIP Trust in his or her will or Living Revocable Trust.

Your LRT might say words to this effect, "If I am the first to die, put the exempted amount into my Bypass Trust. Put the remainder into my QTIP Trust."

Both the Bypass Trust and the QTIP Trust are designed to benefit the spouse for his or her life. They can be designed to give the spouse:

1. All income.
2. Five percent or five thousand (whichever is greater) annually.
3. Anything needed for the spouse's Health, Education, Maintenance and Support.

At the end of the second spouse's life, both the Bypass Trust and the QTIP Trust can go to the persons, institutions or trusts that were originally named by the first decedent.

The beauty of the QTIP Trust is that it can benefit both spouse (as life beneficiary) and other persons or causes (as the ultimate beneficiary). One does not need to choose *between* spouse and others. *Both* can receive appropriate benefits.

THE "SPENDTHRIFT TRUST" ... OR ...
"SAFETY NET TRUST"

1. Who needs it?

Any planner who wants to keep assets from being given away or misspent by the recipient.

2. What does it do?

It keeps assets together "in a pot" and dispenses them, or the income from them, only according to the planner's desires.

In the present state of the American social scene, there are many people who have trouble in the proper care of their resources, particularly their cash resources. In addition to the more traditional problem of people whose money "just goes through their fingers," we have untold numbers of people who suffer from mental stress and disease ... and we have millions who are addicted to alcohol and drugs.

If you have any of these kinds of people in your family, you certainly do not want to give or to leave them substantial sums of money outright. Rather, you need to design some mechanism whereby they may receive a stream of income.

There are two theories of inheritance. One is the "Safety Net" theory ... and one is the "Bonanza" theory. Unfortunately, most bequests follow the bonanza theory. When the parent dies, the child, or other beneficiary, receives a bonanza. Many people are unqualified to properly manage a bonanza.

To assure that your heirs do not receive a bonanza, you have several options, the most useful of which is one that has traditionally been called the "Spendthrift Trust." We usually call it a "Safety Net Trust" because it can be used to provide for heirs if and when they need it.

To create such a trust, you decide on the criteria that you might want designed into it. You might, for example, chose a bank or stockbrokerage trust department as your trustee and instruct that trustee to benefit your children or grandchildren (or both) in these ways:

1. Pay their health insurance premium.
2. Pay their disability insurance premium.

 3. Pay any legitimate educational costs.

 4. Give them all (or part) of the income generated.

With such an approach, you have protected the corpus, or body, of money from being wasted. You have also noted that your values guide the disbursement of your money.

By creating this trust for the benefit of two or three generations ... you might be able to adequately educate many people and to protect all of them from the negative financial aspects of the vicissitudes of life such as poor health or disability.

Some planners create this type of trust and carry it on for many years. At the close of the trust, they give some to heirs and some to charity.

THE CHARITABLE REMAINDER TRUST
1. Who needs it?

Planners who have a taxable estate and who want to make provision for charity at their death (or at some other designated time).
2. What does it do?

It holds assets, pays the income to one or more human beneficiaries ... and eventually pays the body of money to charity.

When a donor wishes to benefit both human beings *and* charitable causes, he can use a charitable trust. The most common such trust is called a charitable remainder trust (CRT). Its name derives from the fact that humans receive the income benefits ... and charity receives the remainder.

In one of its most common forms, the CRT is designed to benefit husband and wife for their lives ... and one or more charitable causes at the death of the last spouse.

Assets are placed into the hands of a Trustee who is directed to pay a percentage, or an amount, to the spouses, generally, every quarter. When the last spouse dies, the Trustee's instructions require him to benefit the charitable causes named in the trust instrument.

The CRT is most useful for donors who have a taxable estate and who have donative intent. In addition to the satisfaction of making a gift to their favored causes, the donors can realize several economic benefits.

When the trust sells assets, it pays no capital gains tax; thus, donors may receive income off of a larger corpus than if they had sold the asset and paid capital gains tax.

By placing assets into a CRT, donors receive an immediate income tax deduction ... even though charity may not benefit for years.

If the donors choose, they can delay the payment of income and, eventually, receive a greater income. This approach creates a retirement plan. When this approach is used, the CRT is sometimes called a Retirement Trust.

The best asset to transfer to a CRT is one that has appreciated in value while owned by the donor.

LIFE INSURANCE
1. Who needs it?

A planner who needs to provide for dependents ... or a planner who wants to purchase life insurance to pay estate taxes.
2. What does it do?

It pays a sum of money to the beneficiary at the death of the insured person.

When a family has a taxable estate, the parents may decide to purchase life insurance in order to pay any death taxes. This might assure the entire family that the next generation would not be forced to sell assets in order to pay those taxes. This approach is especially useful when the family business constitutes a major part of the family's estate.

Naturally, the family would not want to be forced to sell the family business in order to pay taxes. In addition to removing a valuable income-producing asset from the family, a sale, under forced circumstances, might not bring as good a price as it would under more normal conditions.

Enter the life insurance policy. For this particular purpose, the life insurance industry generally promotes a "Last-to-Die" policy. Because there will be no estate tax on the death of the first spouse, there is no need to have the insurance policy pay at that death. The liquidity needs will arise at the death of the second spouse.

Depending on the amount of cash that the family wants to put into the insurance policy, the parents can decide how much of the policy or policies should be in "term" or "cheap" insurance ... and how much should be in "permanent" or "cash value" insurance.

For the best peace of mind, put as much as possible in permanent insurance. Parents may elect to pay off the premium in a short number of years.

A key element in this plan relates to the question of ownership of the policy. There are three offices in each insurance policy:
1.) The Insured
2.) The Owner
3.) The Beneficiary

154

If parents are the owners of the policy, the policy proceeds are in the parents' taxable estate, a condition that you want to avoid.

To make the life insurance work best, be sure that the parents are not the owners of the life insurance policy.

THE LIFE INSURANCE TRUST (LIT)
1. Who needs it?

A planner who has a taxable estate.

2. What does it do?

The LIT is designed to be the owner of the life insurance policy. This process takes it out of the insured's ownership and keeps it out of his taxable estate.

While proceeds from life insurance are not included in a person's taxable income, they are included in a person's taxable estate. To repeat, life insurance proceeds are *not* subject to income tax; but they *are* subject to estate tax.

To understand this possible tax liability, you must understand that each life insurance policy has three offices. They are:

1.) The insured

2.) The owner

3.) The beneficiary

You will readily recognize that the insured and the owner are usually the same person. One person holds two offices. If life insurance is owned by the decedent, the life insurance proceeds are in the taxable estate; hence, a tax may be due.

When people who have a large taxable estate purchase life insurance to pay the tax, they often make the mistake of adding to their taxable estate by the purchase of life insurance.

For example, a widowed man who has a $10,000,000 estate might decide to purchase a $5,000,000 life insurance policy to pay all or most of the federal estate taxes that will be due at his death.

If he takes ownership of that policy (if he holds both the offices of insured and owner), his taxable estate has grown to $15,000,000. The tax bite has grown by about 50%.

However, if he creates a life insurance trust, gives the trust money and lets the trust buy the life insurance policy, the trust is the owner ... and substantial amounts of federal estate tax are saved.

Why? Because the owner doesn't die. The trust doesn't die.

156

THE PERSONAL RESIDENCE TRUST (PRT)
(FORMERLY CALLED "THE GRANTOR RETAINED INCOME TRUST {GRIT}")
1. Who needs it?

Almost nobody.
2. What does it do?

Transfers assets to children at a reduced tax.

Planners wishing to give their home to children or others may find the Personal Residence Trust to be the vehicle of choice. The grantor transfers the home to the trust, lives in the home (hopefully for life), and freezes the value of the home for estate tax purposes.

While this is a widely used procedure, you should be aware that you will, at some future time, have passed the personal residence completely to your offspring. You will no longer own the residence. Under the plan envisioned by those who advocate the use of this trust, you would pay rent to your child once the personal residence had completely passed from your ownership.

Many planners object to the use of this vehicle because they never want to see the parent without ownership of his or her personal residence.

Knowing that a wide variety of life's vicissitudes await most families, many planners fear that a lawsuit against the child who becomes the owner ... might, at some future time, cause the parent to lose his or her residence. Knowledgeable planners fear that the parents might wind up "out in the street."

Given that warning, objectivity demands that the PRT's good points be highlighted.

For a single parent with only one child who is not in a highly litigious profession, the PRT may work very well.

As the purpose of the PRT is to save estate taxes, it should be used, of course, only by families that have a highly taxable estate.

I have never recommended the PRT because I don't like the idea of parents losing their house. If a child becomes the owner ... and, then, that child gets a divorce, the parents may be on the street.

In fairness, I should say that some professional planners think they can avoid that unhappy circumstance.

157

THE LIFE ESTATE DEED
1. Who needs it?

A planner who owns real estate that he wants to pass directly to another person at his death ... and to avoid probate.

2. What does it do?

The Life-Estate Deed passes real estate outside the probate process, directly and instantaneously, at the death of the owner.

Real estate, also called "real property" is usually held by right of a deed. That deed can take many forms.

Many people are using the deed as a means of passing a piece of real estate directly to heirs without the need for probate. You can do this in many ways; but a very popular one is to use the Life-Estate Deed, also sometimes called the Life-Right Deed.

If you want to own the property during your life; but you want it to pass immediately and directly to your son at the time of your death, you may retain a life estate and name the son as remainderman.

If you retain a life estate, that means you own the property as long as you live. When you die, the property immediately belongs to the son ... the remainderman.

You conduct this operation through a deed. You do not use a will or a trust, (unless you want a trust to be the remainderman).

Suppose you wanted your house to go to your daughter and to your grandson; but you did not want your son-in-law to have any ownership of the property. You could:

    1. Retain a life estate for yourself

    2. Give your daughter a consecutive life estate

    3. Make your grandson the remainderman

In this case, you would own it as long as you live. Then, your daughter would own it as long as she lives. In the end, your grandson would own the property.

Suppose you and your wife had married late in life and each of you had children by previous marriages. Assume further that you both put a substantial part of your estate into a house, your residence.

You might choose to take title in a "joint and concurrent life estate" and name several children as the remaindermen.

158

With a "joint and concurrent life estate," you are both owners at this time ... and the survivor of you is the owner for his or her life. No one can "kick you out of your house." The children of each spouse do not receive their ownership until both spouses die.

Many people in second marriages should consider using the joint and concurrent life estate. It protects all parties. Neither member of the elder couple can be "kicked out." All children can receive their share at the second death.

POWER OF ATTORNEY
(BUSINESS POWER OF ATTORNEY)
1. Who needs it?

Almost everybody should name someone to have power of attorney if needed.

2. What does it do?

It allows another person or institution to sign your name to legal documents.

A Power of Attorney (POA) is the power to sign legal documents for another person. This power is greatly misunderstood. Several nuances of the POA need to be understood in order to fit it into your estate plan properly.

It is, first of all, the power to do business for another person. It is not the power over anyone's body. It is power over belongings. In fact, it should be properly called a "Business Power of Attorney."

A POA is good only during the person's life. If and when he dies, the POA is extinguished. Do not think that a POA is a substitute for your will. When the person dies, the POA is invalidated; it has become extinct.

A POA has two dimensions; it has breadth ... and it has depth. Let's look at breadth first; if it is a "General" POA, it is broad as the equator. It covers everything. If a general POA does not state a starting point, it becomes operable immediately. Give someone your general power of attorney without stating a starting point, and that person can go waste all your assets right now.

Enter the concept of "Springing." A POA can spring from a certain event. For example, someone could give you his power of attorney and say that it comes into being or springs into being only when he embarks on an International Air Plane Flight.

Or he could make it spring from this event: "If two board-certified physicians determine that I am incapable of taking care of my affairs and so state in writing, this POA springs into being."

If you want the POA to be less than a general power of attorney, you might decide to limit it and to thus make it a "Limited Power of Attorney." If you were moving to another city and had found a house you wanted to buy, you might give someone your limited power of attorney to buy the house and to sign all relevant papers while you are in the process of moving your family and household goods.

In addition to breadth, a POA has depth. If a power of attorney does not state otherwise, it is extinguished when you become disabled. If you want the POA to "endure" your disability, you can make it a "durable" power of attorney. Most POAs written in recent times are, indeed, Durable Powers of Attorney.

Do you need a POA if you have a Living Revocable Trust (LRT) and have named a Standby Trustee to take over in case of your disability? Yes. You still need a POA because you may have ownership of items that are not in your LRT and, hence, not under the power of the Standby Trustee.

In addition to a POA, you need a Medical Power of Attorney (MPOA) that tells what medical procedures you would want done if you were not of a disposing mind. Many states have combined the MPOA with a Living Will. Still others call the documents related to this issue an Advanced Medical Directive. Consult local legal counsel to see exactly which documents you need in your state.

"PAY-ON-DEATH" BANK ACCOUNT
1. Who needs it?

A bank account owner or owners who want that account to vest only in himself/themselves during life; but at death to belong to another person.
2. What does it do?

It keeps assets out of the attachable estate of heirs until death of the bank account owner; but, at owner's death, the heirs own the account immediately.

A bank account can be designed to belong to one person during his or her life and, subsequently, to pay to another person, trust or institution ... at the death of the original owner. Such an account is often called a Pay-on-Death (POD) bank account.

In many instances, this is an excellent estate planning device.

Suppose that you have a substantial savings account and that you have one heir that you want to receive that account at your death. You merely go to the bank and tell the officer that you want to own the account during your life ... but that you want a certain person, whom you then name, to be the owner when you die.

The bank officer will give you the proper documentation, generally at no cost.

Unfortunately, many planners are unaware of the POD account. Consequently, they often endanger their assets by using other means. Often, they place their children's names on bank accounts as joint owners.

While joint ownership may be desirable in many instances, it has one major drawback. If your child, the other joint owner, were to be sued and if a judgment were granted against your child, your bank account could be at risk.

It is often better to use the POD account than to use joint ownership. With the POD account, the second owner has no legal interest in the account as long as the first owner is alive. Having no legal interest in the account, the second owner cannot lose the account to a lawsuit during the first owner's life.

THE CRUMMEY TRUST
1. Who needs it?

A person who wants to place assets into a trust for heirs and to take advantage of his annual exclusion from taxation.
2. What does it do?

When a parent, or any other person, makes a gift to another person, that gift must be a "gift of present interest" if it is to qualify to be an annual exclusion (from taxation) gift.

In other words, if you are trying to use your annual exclusion from taxation, the gift must be a gift of present interest. It must be an outright present gift. The person must be able to go out and spend the gift that minute.

Sometimes, a parent may want to put money into a trust for the future benefit of children or grandchildren. The parent may want to transfer money into a trust and state that the money is for college education ... or for some other future benefit.

When such a gift is made, it is a gift of future interest and the gift does not qualify for the annual exclusion from gift taxation. Gift tax must be paid.

Enter the Crummey Trust, a trust named for the man who invented it.

He wanted to make gifts for the future benefit of family members and, after consultation with his attorney, decided to create a short-term trust in which the money would lose its "future interest" characteristics.

He created an instrument, the Crummey Trust, into which the funds would be temporarily deposited. When the money is put into the Crummey Trust, the donee is notified that the money is there and that he can come and get the money if he so desires.

But if he does not lay claim to the money within a specified time frame, the money moves on into the permanent trust where is will serve a future benefit to the donee.

Of course, children or grandchildren recognize that the parent donor is doing them a favor and that he may continue to do that every year if they cooperate. They do not usually come and get the money. They allow it to serve the future interest.

Fortunately for the Crummey family ... and for all successive ones who wish to make gifts of future interest, the IRS approved the Crummey Trust ... and stated that a gift so treated would be deemed to qualify for the annual exclusion from taxation.

Therefore, the Crummey Trust, also called Crummey Power, has come to be a standard means of converting a gift of future interest into a gift of present interest.

YOUR TAX-DEFERRED RETIREMENT PLAN
1. Who needs it?

Planners who want to defer tax on some of their income will want to deposit some money into a retirement plan.

2. What does it do?

A Retirement Plan defers income tax until the money is taken out of the plan, usually in retirement years.

Because of the outstanding tax benefits granted to those who use IRAs, 401ks, 403bs, and other "qualified pension plans," these instruments have become very popular. Here, for purposes of convenience, we will refer to all these plans as IRAs.

Most funds in these plans avoided income tax when they were placed into the fund ... and they grow tax-free.

With rare exceptions, the IRA is such an outstanding device that we want to keep the money in it as long as possible, drawing money out only when we are forced, by circumstances or government rules, to do so.

Do not put your IRA into a Living Revocable Trust. To place it into the trust, you must first remove the funds from the IRA, pay income taxes ... and then place the funds into the LRT. Also, be wary of those who would advise you to remove funds from your IRA to purchase insurance. Again, you have created a taxable event when you take funds out of the IRA.

The IRA, when passing to a named beneficiary (person, trust or institution), does not go through probate.

But, at your death, the funds can be highly taxed. They can be subject to state and federal income tax, state and federal death taxes and federal excise taxes. In many instances, IRA funds have been depleted by more than 75%.

If the IRA names your spouse as a beneficiary, he or she can create a "Spousal Roll-Over IRA" and transfer the funds to that instrument without payment of any tax. The income is then taxed when he or she takes income.

But again, the death taxes can be substantial when the spouse dies.

YOUR LIFETIME RETIREMENT PLAN: THE "POP" OPTION
(PENSION OPTIMIZATION PLAN)

1. Who needs it?

Workers who have earned a pension that pays for their life or, at a reduced rate, for the life of worker and spouse.

2. What does it do?

Advocates claim that the family will have more money if the worker takes the largest possible pension and uses part of the money to purchase life insurance.

Many federal employees ... and others who have similar pension plans ... have the option of either:

1. Taking the pension only for their life

or

2. Taking a smaller pension for their life; but including their spouse's life in the length of the pension

Generally, the pension for the surviving spouse amounts to only about 60% of the pension drawn during the life of the worker who earned the it.

Let's say that the federal worker, in this case, a man, can draw a pension of $4,000 per month for his life.

or

He can draw $3,000 per month for his life and, if his spouse survives him, she can draw about $2,000 for her life after he dies.

Choosing between the two options is often difficult.

Enter the "Pension Optimization Plan (POP)."

Many planners advocate the pension optimization plan. By the way, they ... not this writer ... gave it the name by which it has come to be known.

Advocates of the POP say the better approach is for the federal worker to take the largest dollar amount he can for his life ... and to purchase life insurance that will pay out to his wife at his death. In this case, they would advocate his taking the entire $4,000 per month. They would say that he will have plenty of money to live on and to purchase life insurance.

166

The POP advocates will sit down with the federal worker and try to show him that he will have more money during his life and that he will provide adequately for his wife if he adopts the POP.

Adopting the POP does not end his decision-making process. He still must decide how much insurance to purchase and exactly how he wants to pay for it.

The POP is offered here as one option that people in these circumstance should consider. Careful consideration should precede the adoption of the POP.

It is easy for you to see that the life insurance industry is the one that created the POP. Almost every life insurance agent is a POP advocate.

THE FAMILY LIMITED PARTNERSHIP
1. Who needs it?

A family that owns investment real estate or a business.

2. What does it do?

It "divides" the asset into small pieces (partnership shares) that can be given or sold.

For families who own substantial investment real estate holdings, the family limited partnership is an excellent estate planning device. Used properly in a highly taxable estate, this instrument can save the family many thousands of dollars in gift and estate taxes.

In a limited partnership, there are two kinds of partners: general and limited. The general partner or partners have all the management responsibility of the business. By definition, a limited partner cannot participate in the management of the business.

Limited partners, while not having the benefit of management, do have a wonderful benefit. They are responsible for the debts and losses of the partnership only to the extent of their limited partnership interest. If they have $10,000 invested, that is all they could lose.

To save gift and estate taxes, the parents will create the partnership and transfer some asset, perhaps a tract of land, into it. Then the parents will be both general and limited partners at the beginning.

Let's say that the land is worth $1 million, and for this example, say that it is not increasing in value.

After creating the partnership, the parents begin an annual gifting program to each of the children. While the parents will want to keep the general partner shares in order to retain control, they can give the limited partner shares away and lose no control.

With each of 100 partnership shares being worth $10,000, the parents can give one percent per year to each child from each parent. This procedure passes "white money," i.e. partnership shares out of the parents' taxable estate ... and places them into the children's (or grandchildren's) ownership.

The theory behind this approach is that it delays the taxation on the asset for a generation (or two generations). With each generation being about 25 years younger than the previous one, this strategy delays tax by 25 years for each generation to whom gifts are given.

Let me emphasize that this device is used for investment real estate; it is *not* very useful with residential property.

Farm families and real estate investors should consider the use of the family limited partnership. It is vastly under-utilized. Consequently, many families pay far too much tax.

FUN QUIZ

CHAPTERS ONE THROUGH TWELVE

1. T F When one has a Living Revocable Trust,
he must place his IRA into it.

2. T F If an irrevocable trust pays income to heirs,
they, not the trust, pay the income tax.

3. T F When you write a will, you must record it at
the courthouse.

4. T F A charitable trust can pay you income for life.

5. T F The Executor or Trustee writes a big check to the
IRS when he funds the Bypass Trust.

6. T F Capital gains tax is owed when one inherits property.

7. T F Some states impose a state inheritance tax.

8. T F A Limited Partner manages the partnership.

9. T F A "consecutive life estate" refers to a prison term.

10. T F A "Last-to-die" insurance policy pays only when both
of the insured people die.

Test answers are shown on Page 223.

CHAPTER THIRTEEN

ESTATE PLANNING STRATEGIES

There are many different strategies that may be used in an estate plan. In addition to learning the kinds of documents that you can use, you need to learn the means of implementing the documents and the various tactics that can be used. In essence, the strategies serve the purpose of tying the various documents together so that the estate plan becomes a meaningful whole.

To help you learn these strategies, I have listed and commented on several of them in this chapter. Even though you will not use all of them, you need to have a basic understanding of each of them so that you know why you are .. or are not ... using a given strategy.

ALLOWING YOUR ESTATE TO PASS BY
YOUR STATE'S LAWS OF INTESTACY

"If you choose to write no will,
the state will write one for you."

Each state has a set of laws that determine how "personally owned" assets will pass if the decedent has no will. These laws are called by various names such as:

"The laws of descent and distribution."

"The laws of intestate succession."

"The laws of intestacy."

While the superficial observer might take umbrage at these laws, they do serve a worthwhile purpose. They keep personally owned assets in the family if the decedent has made no provision for passing them.

These laws are not quite as dictatorial as they might appear on first glance. They apply only to those assets that would have passed by a will had the decedent written one. They do not apply to assets transferred to revocable trusts, to assets owned jointly or to assets owned in some form of life estate.

They apply only to assets that would have passed by will if the decedent had caused a valid will to have been written.

A typical set of intestacy laws might have a section that states:

"If the decedent is survived by a spouse and descendants of decedent and a prior
relationship, 50% of the estate goes to the spouse and 50% to the descendants."

Of course, each state's laws are slightly different; so do not take the preceding paragraph to be definitive for your case. It is presented here only for purposes of illustration.

In the early days of my estate planning seminar productions, I would place a slide up on the screen that listed several of the sections from one of the states' laws of intestacy.

When I did so, I was always somewhat amazed at the rapt attention of the audience and of the almost unanimous copious note-taking.

Actually, an informed person should give little or no attention to state's laws of intestacy because he or she will *not* allow his estate to pass in that manner. An enlightened person will use one or more estate planning strategies to ascertain that the "state's will" has no effect.

Do not depend on your state's laws of intestacy. Be a pro-active planner and be sure that you make your dispositive decisions. Do not allow the state to make them for you.

THE WIDOW'S ELECTION

In order to be sure that no widow was ever completely disinherited by her husband, many states have created a law that gives the widow the election to take part of the estate. However, this is an active ... not a passive ... decision that the widow must make.

If your spouse has completely disinherited you, you can go to the probate court and file a widow's election.

In most states, this tactic will give you the right to receive a certain portion of the estate. Generally, this portion is between one-third and one-half of the estate. In some states, the portion awarded to the widow depends on the number of children that the decedent had.

Note that this award is *not* completely automatic. One often hears that a widow "automatically" receives a certain portion of the estate. That statement is not correct. You do not receive it automatically. You must make the effort to file the widow's election.

Generally, the widow's election pertains only to those items in the probatable estate. It includes only those items that pass from the will. It would not, in most cases, include a house that the decedent owned jointly with some other person.

Neither would it include a bank account owned jointly. Insurance proceeds are also, generally, outside the widow's election as are pension plan proceeds.

If and when you ... or a friend, ever experiences a spousal disinheritance, proceed immediately to an estate planning attorney licensed to practice in your state and engage him or her to act for you ... to claim the Widow's Election.

SHRINKING THE ESTATE

For families that have a taxable estate and that own large real estate holdings, there is an excellent estate planning device known as "shrinking" the estate.

Suppose the parents own a tract of investment land worth $1 million and that they decide to form a family limited partnership and to place the land into the partnership. They will then make gifts of partnership shares to as many of their family members as they choose.

Ideally, they will use their annual exclusion from taxation, $10,000 per year, to move the value of partnership shares out of their taxable estate.

If the partnership had 100 shares, each share of the $1 million asset would be worth $10,000.

If father, however, gives a daughter one share ... and she proceeds to offer to sell that share to a non-family-member investor, ... that investor is likely to reply to this offer by saying,

"I realize that this share is worth $10,000 to you because you are a family member; but it is worth less to me because I will not be in control of the partnership. Having no control, I will be unable to market it easily. I will have no general partner interest. The parents will retain control, as general partners. Therefore, I will offer only $6,700 for the share."

Because $6,700 is the best price you can get for the share on the open market, the value of that share ... and of each share in the partnership ... has just decreased by one-third. Each share has just *shrunk* ... for estate and gift taxation purposes.

You have shrunk the estate.

Knowing that this is a likely scenario, estate planners have adopted a method of shrinking the value of each share ... and hence, the value of the entire asset, for gift tax purposes. In this example, the land that was worth $1 million for gifting purposes is now worth only $670,000.

The value of the estate has shrunk as far as the tax man is concerned.

You can happily report to your spouse, ...
"Honey, I shrunk the estate."

CHOOSING A TRUSTEE

You may choose any person you want as a trustee of most trusts. You cannot choose yourself or your spouse for some trusts; but, in general, you may choose any human being.

Also, you may choose any corporation licensed to be a trustee in the state where you live. For the most part, the following can be used:

1. Banks
2. Stockbrokerages
3. Independent Trust Companies

Often planners ask me if it would be wise to choose a lawyer or accountant as trustee. Because the foregoing three kinds of companies are the only ones licensed by your state, you can choose one or more of your advisors, acting as a personal human being; but you *cannot* choose his firm if it is a corporation and is not state-licensed to be a trustee.

If you decide to choose an individual human being as trustee, be sure to choose one or more "standby" trustees who will act if your chosen trustee is unable or unwilling to act.

Which is better? Individual or corporation?

Usually, you are more knowledgeable of an individual and may be more comfortable with this choice.

However, individuals are not, generally, bonded.

If you choose an individual and that individual's secretary runs off with your money, you have lost everything.

If, on the other hand, a corporate trustee's employee were dishonest, that trustee is bonded ... and the bonding company replaces the money.

Can you bond an individual?

Yes. The bond must be renewed annually and the premium must be paid each year. If your individual trustee should ever forget to pay the bonding premium, your trust might be at risk. In general, corporate trustees, while not perfect, are better than individual trustees.

SPRINKLING POWERS

A wonderful and useful tool that can be used in trusts is that of ...
Sprinkling Powers.

Using Sprinkling Powers, or Spraying Powers, when designing a
trust for your children or grandchildren can help "even out" the
benefits for the family when one heir may have, from other sources, far
more ... or far less than other heirs.

You simply give your trustee sprinkling powers over a certain
amount of money or over the income from a certain fund.

For example, many counselees have told me that they would like
to "even out" the inheritance because they are sure that one of their
children is going to receive far more benefit from in-laws ... than is
another heir.

When this is the case ... and when a parent is leaving a trust for the
benefit of his or her children/grandchildren, I often recommend
Sprinkling Powers for the Trustee. If the Trustee is to give the income
to the heirs each year, we might say,

"I give my Trustee Sprinkling Powers over the income to
make each child's situation more equitable. The Trustee may
give one child as much as 70% of the income if that child
receives far less from other sources."

Given these powers, the Trustee might ask each heir to show him
a copy of their annual tax return. With tax information in hand, he
could decide how to sprinkle the income.

Granted, this method may be a bit awkward; and I am not
necessarily recommending it. My purpose here is merely to show you
that you have the choice of using this strategy ... and that a number of
ways exist for you to use your Sprinkling Powers.

MAKING GIFTS TO HEIRS DURING LIFE

Even though the annual exclusion of $10,000 from each donor to as many donees as he or she may choose is widely known, it is poorly used. In addition, few people know that they can use their $600,000 lifetime exemption during life; consequently, vast amounts of tax are paid on assets that could have been easily shielded.

At one of my Maryland seminars, a prosperous, well-known businessman attended and, after the seminar, came up to me and said, "Dan, my estate plan isn't worth a darn. Would you come back and let me bring my kids together so you can help us all with some estate planning?"

We arranged the meeting and his four children all attended. In addition, several executives from the businessman's firm were invited to participate.

Having a highly taxable estate, the businessman told me that he had given each of his four children stock in his business which had appreciated in their estates to the point that each child now had stock worth $10 million.

Each of his children was married and each had two children.

The stock had appreciated, for the last three years, at the rate of 24% per year. By every indication, it would continue to grow at a healthy pace.

I asked if the four children had made gifts to their children.

"No," he replied. "How will that help us?"

I explained that each of his children could give to their children, or to a trust for their children, at the present time ... and that this strategy would place the growth of the stock into the estates of the grandchildren. In other words, it would be taxed at about 25 years later than the children's estates.

"How much can they give?" he asked.

Each of the four children could move a total of $1,240,000 the first year; $40,000 each year thereafter with no tax obligation.

Here's how.

Each of the four could give his or her lifetime exemption amount of $600,000. They could then give their spouse an equal amount and he/she could give the additional $600,000 to the children.

Each couple could move $1.2 million out of their taxable estates just by using their lifetime exemptions during life. Remember, the lifetime exemption amount can be given in life or left as a legacy at death. It is usable *in life or death*.

Then the businessmen's children could give $40,000 as annual exclusion gifts. By having their spouses sign a gift tax return noting that the $10,000 annual exclusion gift was being given to each child from each parent's exclusion, a couple with two children can give $40,000 each year to their two children with no tax obligation.

In summary, each of the four children and his/her spouse could give:

1. Husband's lifetime exemption ...	$ 600,000
2. Wife's lifetime exemption	$ 600,000
3. Husband's two annual exclusions ...	$ 20,000
4. Wife's two annual exclusions ...	$ 20,000
TOTAL	$1,240,000

After I explained this procedure to the businessman, he replied, "We've been paying $400 per hour to a New York firm for estate planning advice and have not been told of this means of tax avoidance.

"Up till now, I thought the $600,000 lifetime exemption could be used only at death."

In this case, the gifts would be gifts of stock. Gifts could be, of course, gifts of cash, partnership shares or anything else of value.

After using the gift of $1,240,000 in the first year, each couple would continue giving to a trust for their children each year. They could give $40,000 each year by using their $10,000 annual exclusions from taxation ... and have no gift tax liability.

Making gifts to heirs during life is an excellent estate planning device ... and should be used by many more planners.

Remember, each gift of $10,000 can save as much as $5,500 in federal gift tax.

Also, remember that it is wise to use your lifetime exemption of $600,000 during life under certain circumstances.

MAKING GIFTS TO HEIRS
(WHEN YOU ANTICIPATE
LARGE GROWTH IN YOUR ESTATE)

In Vermont, a building contractor told me he had an estate of $17 million and he anticipated a large growth in the next few years.

He said, "My wife and I want to do everything possible for our three children now. What should we do?"

I suggested that they set up a trust for the children and give that trust all they could give at this time without payment of taxes.

Not having used their lifetime exemptions of $600,000 each, the two of them could give the trust $1.2 million. In addition, they could each use their annual exclusions of $10,000 per donee ... a total of $60,000 per year from the two parents.

I recommended that he set up a trust for the benefit (FBO) of the children, immediately giving it $1,260,000. No tax would be due.

Here's how the $1,260,000 would be counted.

1. Husband's lifetime exemption	$ 600,000
2. Wife's lifetime exemption	$ 600,000
3. Husband's three annual exclusions	$ 30,000
4. Wife's three annual exclusions	$ 30,000
TOTAL	$1,260,000

Each year thereafter, they could give the trust $60,000 by using their annual exclusions from taxation.

When you expect growth in your taxable estate, it is wise to consider moving as much as possible out of that estate via lifetime gifts to people or to trusts.

USING THE UNIFORM GIFTS TO MINORS ACT

A popular method of providing education funds for children and grandchildren is the use of the Gifts to Minors Act account. Many grandparents are using this method of helping their families educate future generations.

But gifts given under this act have one great negative aspect. The total gift, no matter how large, becomes the property of the minor when he reaches the age of majority, age 18 in most states.

A grandmother approached me during the seminar break in Nashville, Tennessee, where I was sponsored by the Baptist Hospital and where I worked with its chief development official, George Bennett. She said,

"Be sure to tell people *not* to use
the Uniform Gift to Minors Act."

Then she related this story, "My husband and I were advised to use it to make gifts to our grandchildren for their college education. Now they are 16 and 17 years of age ... and they just can't wait to spend all their money on new cars and fast living as soon as they reach age 18.

"They have no desire to improve their minds; they have no intention of using the money for education. All they can think about is the good time they will have when they reach age 18 and get their money."

Concluding, she said, "I wish we had never given money to those accounts."

She regretted having used the Gifts to Minors Act accounts.

There are two far-better approaches for grandparents who want to contribute to their grandchildren's education:

1. Don't make gifts of any kind to the grandchildren during their age of minority.

or

2. Create a Safety Net Trust and make gifts to it ... for benefit of the grandchildren.

If you use choice number one and make no gifts during their minority, you can keep your money and invest it as you please. When they are ready for college, you can make tuition payments to the college

181

and can still give the grandchild a tax-free additional amount of as much as $10,000 per year by using your annual exclusion from taxation.

Actually, you can give more than that by using part of your $600,000 lifetime exemption from taxation.

If you use choice number two and create a Safety Net Trust, you can give the trustee explicit instructions as to how the money is to be used. You can be sure that your money will not be used for non-productive purposes.

You might, for example, instruct the trustee to pay "room, board, books, tuition, health needs and reasonable transportation costs." With these words, you are giving your trustee adequate leeway to make good decisions; but you are guaranteeing that your trust will not be spent on foolish luxuries.

Either of the two above-named strategies is far better than using the Uniform Gifts to Minors Act account.

"But," you say, "we have already set up a Uniform Gifts to Minors Act account and have made substantial deposits to it. Should we continue?"

No. Do *not* continue to make gifts to the account.

Quit ! !

Stop ! !

You cannot extract the gifts from the account. You must keep them in the account until the minor reaches the age of majority. Don't compound the problem by adding to the account.

Create a trust and begin making your additional deposits to the trust instead of to the Minors Act account.

USING "PER STIRPES" OR "PER CAPITA"

In almost every will that is shown to me in estate planning sessions, there appears the term "per stirpes." In hundreds of such sessions, I have yet to find a counselee who understands what it means. It is one of the most misunderstood terms in all jurisprudence.

The two terms "per stirpes" and "per capita" are antithetical. They mean just the opposite of each other.

A will, or other document, usually has one or the other term used at least one time.

"Per stirpes" means "in place of." It means that the grandchildren are "in place of" the children. As contingent beneficiaries, the grandchildren are "in place of" their parents, the children of the grandparents in whose documents the term appears.

"Per capita" means "by head" or "per head."

If the "normal" line of succession pertains, the terms have *no effect*. If each successive generation dies in the natural or sequential order, these terms are *not operative*.

Repeat: In most families, these terms *never* come into play. They are included in the document only as a contingency or back-up to the normal course of events.

Only if the testator's (will-maker's) children predecease him do the terms apply. Only if his children die before he dies do the two terms have any applicability.

If an "out of order" or non-sequential death occurs, the procedure governed by these terms becomes operational.

An effective illustration might look like this:

Suppose you have two children, Ann and Ben.

Ann has *one* child.

Ben has *ten* children.

You have *eleven* grandchildren.

If your will says that Ann and Ben are to inherit your estate "per stirpes," it means this:

"If either of my children die before I die, each set of grandchildren is to receive, equally, the one half of my estate inheritance that my child would have received had he not died early."

If both Ann and Ben predecease you, Ann's child gets *half* of your estate and Ben's children get *half, divided among them*; they each receive only five percent of the estate.

Ann's child gets ten times as much as does each of Ben's children.

If, on the other hand, your will says that Ann and Ben are to inherit your estate "per capita," ... and if Ann and Ben predecease you, each grandchild receives one-eleventh of your estate because they inherit "per capita" or "by head."

Must you choose either one of these alternatives?

Not necessarily. You might leave your entire estate to a trust for the grandchildren. In that case, you would say, "I am leaving this trust to a class of people, my grandchildren."

To be sure that you do not trigger Generation Skipping Transfer Tax (GSTT), do not allow your estate to give the grandchildren more than $1 million. Each grandparent has a $1 million exemption from GSTT. Be sure that you understand your exemption and that you use it properly.

The trust for grandchildren is a much better approach in most cases than is either the "per capita" or "per stirpes" technique.

DISCLAIMING
A GREAT STRATEGY ... A POOR PLAN

When a person is named in a will or other dispositive document to receive any asset, he has the right to disclaim the asset; he can simply say, "I don't want it and I refuse to accept it."

On the surface, this appears to be a foolhardy response; it appears to be a stupid thing to do.

But, in certain cases, it can be an extremely intelligent strategy.

In Montgomery, Alabama, where I have worked with Paul Alexander of the Baptist Hospital for several years, I was invited out to the new office of a physician who wanted some advice regarding his estate plan.

The doctor told me that he and his wife had a combined estate of approximately $10 million.

"One of the problems that I see on the horizon," he noted, "is that both my mother and my wife's mother have substantial estates. I remember you showed us, in your seminar, the cascading effect of passing one taxable estate into another can create higher tax bills for the family."

"That is certainly true," I replied. "Many families pay tax on the same estate more than one time."

"Well," he went on, "both our mothers have estates of nearly $2 million each. Do we want them to leave assets to my wife and me? Or, do we want them to do more for our children?"

I explained that the older generation can, if it so chooses, skip generations with limited amounts of money without the payment of Generation Skipping Transfer Tax (GSTT); I told him the limit is currently $1 million.

"So," I said, "a mother could create an estate plan that would allow as much as $1 million to completely skip you and your wife. It could go directly to your children ... or to a trust for your children."

He said, "Both mothers are getting on up there in years. I doubt that we could explain this to them. Is there any other way?"

"Yes," I said. "You and/or your wife could disclaim some of your inheritance. If your children are next in line to receive it, your disclaiming action would cause the asset to go directly to them."

He was pleased to learn of this approach and noted it.

To his credit, he did not think of the disclaimer as a substitute for good planning. He recognized it as a strategy to be used when it is impossible to implement an intelligent plan.

On the other hand, a woman came to see me in Garden City, New York, and told me that her lawyer had told her not to worry about a similar situation. He advised her she did not need a sophisticated estate plan because, when the time came, her heirs could simply disclaim the inheritance.

I call this "The Lazy Man's Estate Plan."

It might also be called "The Stupid Attorney's Estate Plan."

As a planning strategy, the disclaimer is a poor estate planning device.

Why?

Because so many things can go wrong in the intended process; things like these:

1. To disclaim properly, you must not touch a penny of the inheritance until the disclaiming process is complete.

Suppose that your father died and that he had a checking account into which he had deposited all the money ... and on which he had placed your name as a joint owner.

Because you are a joint owner, you can use the money at any time while he is living; and you own the account outright once he has passed away.

At his death, you call your children across the country to tell them that their grandfather died. You tell them, "I know he would want me to write a check to pay for the airfare for you kids to attend the funeral." You write the check out of the aforementioned account.

Later, you wish to disclaim the inheritance you received in favor of your children.

Your action of writing one check out of the account may have disallowed the use of the disclaimer. Writing the check could completely upset your desired plan.

2. If you plan to disclaim, you will need to work very closely with the attorneys and accountants who told you about this strategy and who expect to help you implement it.

What if one of them was on a three-month trip to Europe? What if they died? What if you moved to another state and took the concept into the office of a professional who did not know your plans ... or who did not know how to disclaim?

The bottom line is that disclaiming is a good strategy to be used when no really good plan has been adopted. But it is an abhorrent estate planning device and should never be a part of your plan. It is only to be used in an emergency.

Disclaiming is a good tool to use in an emergency.

Disclaiming is *not* a good estate planning strategy on which to depend.

SPLITTING THE ESTATE

When planning a taxable estate for a married couple, splitting the estate is usually a desirable strategy.

If your estate is now at the $600,000 level ... or if it will be at that level at the death of the first spouse, you can achieve significant tax savings by splitting the estate and by implementing the Bypass Trust.

Each individual has a lifetime exemption from taxation of $600,000. To use this exemption twice ... once for husband and once for wife, a rather detailed plan must be established.

While, on the surface, the $600,000 exemption per individual appears to be quite simple, it is not automatic. To repeat, you do *not* automatically receive two $600,000 exemptions per married couple.

Because the vast majority of married couples own many of their assets jointly, many families *waste* one of the two potential lifetime exemptions.

If husband and wife have a total estate of $1.2 million ... and if they own all assets jointly, they are apt to lose one of the lifetime exemptions. If husband dies while they own everything jointly, all the assets immediately become the wife's property.

Because this approach is simple and easy, many couples think it is the best option.

But this procedure wastes one of the lifetime exemptions.

As a result of the immediate transfer to the wife via joint ownership, the husband's estate does not use his lifetime exemption. Of course, due to the spousal rule that says "no tax on spousal transfers," there is no tax at this point. However, if the wife dies next year, she has a taxable estate of $1.2 million and her estate has the use of only one lifetime exemption of $600,000.

The second $600,000 is, in effect, taxed. The tax bill is *$235,000*.

A better approach is to split the estate into two separate ones of $600,000 for him and $600,000 for her. By splitting the estate ... and by implementing a plan that calls for the use of the Bypass Trust, the family saves that $235,000 in tax.

188

Here's how.

At the first death, we "pay all the tax that is due on the first estate" and, of course, that tax is zero.

The great feature of "paying all the tax that is due," is ... this estate can never be taxed again. We have, in effect, paid all the tax that will ever be due.

Of course, the surviving spouse has the use of the first $600,000 for his/her entire life.

If the second spouse dies next year, with an taxable estate of $600,000, there is no tax. To repeat, this strategy saves $235,000.

"How can we split the estate? How can we split the house?" is a question we often hear.

By using a form of ownership called "Tenants in Common" ownership, each spouse can own an undivided half of the house. If the house is worth $600,000 and it is owned "Tenants in Common," each spouse has $300,000 worth of house in his/her estate.

The best approach is for each spouse to have a Living Revocable Trust ... and for that trust to own that spouse's half of the Tenancy in Common.

Most couples who anticipate an at-death estate of $600,000 or more should split the estate.

WRITING A PREMARITAL AGREEMENT

On several occasions, I have met people who thought their estate planning problems were solved because they had written a premarital agreement.

In most cases, they are wrong.

Almost every premarital agreement is worth only the cost of the paper on which it is written, less the cost of erasure.

In December, 1996, USA Television Network ran a feature hour-long program on the life of Doris Duke, heiress to the Duke fortune. According to the program, Doris, only one hour prior to her second marriage, handed her new husband-to-be a premarital agreement and insisted that he sign.

Evidently, he felt enough pressure to sign; so, he did.

According to the USA feature, they later divorced ... and he received $25,000 per year for life. Of course, this allowance constituted less than the interest payment on her, eventual $1.2 billion estate.

While the details of their relationship are not, for our present purposes, relevant, the general lesson in estate planning is both relevant and didactic.

This story reminds us that most premarital agreements were presented in just about this same manner, abruptly, surprisingly and without the advice of independent counsel for both parties.

In addition, most premarital agreements fail to provide each party with complete detailed information regarding the total net worth of the estate of each party. Many states require this disclosure in order for a premarital agreement to be enforceable.

When one of the Mars candy heirs married for the second time, she used her first married name and did not indicate to the husband-to-be that she was a Mars family member ... and that her net worth exceeded three billion dollars.

Later, when they divorced, he sued against the premarital agreement on the basis that New Jersey law required full disclosure of all assets in order for the premarital agreement to be enforceable.

His lawsuit contended that "she did not fully disclose her net worth in the agreement; therefore, it is null and void."

The main point I wish to emphasize is that these agreements are quite technical and that they require careful and cooperative planning in addition to the assistance of experienced and specialized legal counsel.

Please, Mother or Father, do not think that you have solved your estate plan just because you have insisted that your daughter have a premarital agreement.

Most of the premarital agreements I have seen are so easy to overturn, they are actually *laughable*.

A better approach for the mother who wants to be sure her estate does not wind up in the hands of a son-in-law is to use an irrevocable trust. We generally use the Safety Net Trust.

The trust is better than the premarital agreement.

Neither parents not the principles should depend on a premarital agreement. Most of them are worthless.

USING THE "MOVE" CLAUSE

One of the great stumbling blocks to a good estate plan is the fact that people cannot settle on a trustee. Even after they have recognized the need for a trust, the majority of people have difficulty in trustee selection. Many people fail to implement their plan simply because they cannot decide on the person or institution they want for their trustee.

While trust departments are not perfect, they are far better than most human beings. Our general advice to those we counsel is they should select a trust department as trustee for any long-term irrevocable trust. (A person can serve as his own trustee, in nearly every state, for a Living Revocable Trust.)

"But," we often hear, "I know a trust company that did a poor job for my uncle's trust. I am hesitant to name a bank or stockbrokerage trust department as the trustee of my family trust."

The answer to this dilemma is "The Move Clause."

We generally recommend that the trustor put these words into any long-term irrevocable trust:

"If my adult heirs, by a majority vote, ever choose to move the trust from this trust department to any other trust department authorized to do trust business in the state of _____, they may do so."

By using this paragraph in your trust, you are assuring yourself and your family that none of you will ever be placed "under the thumb" of an irresponsible or truculent trustee. While the family cannot reach in and remove the money from the trust, they can *move* the trust to any other trust company in the state.

On the surface, it might appear that the bank trust department would not approve of this clause. You might be surprised. While working with a trust officer one day in 1996, this subject came up.

The trust officer said, "We like to see that clause in trusts." He went on to explain, "We don't want anyone to feel they are bound to us. We want to work hard and to do a good job on all our trusts so that the families will want to keep the trust with us. We think they will be more comfortable knowing they can move the trust if they want to."

Already having great respect for the particular bank he represented and for him personally, I increased my regard for both. He and his bank could see that good customer service is never poor business.

Advise your attorney to use the move clause.

KEEPING GOVERNMENT BENEFITS
FOR A MENTALLY ILL SON

A couple in their 70s, came to see me and told me a heart-wrenching story.

"About 40 years ago, we adopted two small boys," the husband said.

"When one was 19, he developed mental problems and has been in and out of the state hospital for the last 20 years."

His wife added, "He receives Supplemental Security Income (SSI) government benefits ... and we help some."

Looking down, the man continued, "Our other son is some kind of Hell's Angel.

"We hear from him about once or twice a year from wherever he is hanging out ... and he has never held a job for very long."

The lady said, "We have an estate of $400,000 and we are so worried that it will be wasted and that all our hard work will go for nothing."

The gentleman took up her thought, "On the one hand, we don't want our assets to replace the government money that our mentally-ill son receives. On the other hand, we know that our 'Hell's Angel' son would just waste the money on a lifestyle of which we disapprove.

"We just don't know what to do."

I showed them how to create a Safety Net Trust (SNT) that would keep the principal intact ... and out of the hands of either of the sons. I explained that we could add "luxury" features that would allow the disabled son to continue receiving SSI payments.

When children are receiving these SSI government benefits, we often use the luxury features to assure that their basic needs will be met by their government stipend. Then the trust can assist with the small "luxuries" that can help make their life less difficult.

When we finished our conference, I offered to go to the lawyer with them to explain everything. We arranged a meeting time at his office. He agreed with my recommendations and drafted the suggested documents.

At the conclusion of our session in the lawyer's office, the lady turned to her husband and exclaimed,

"It's a miracle."

At that point I realized how traumatized they had been over these circumstances. While the plan we created was far from miraculous to us, it lifted such a heavy burden from their shoulders that the woman considered it a miracle.

KEEPING $2 MILLION SECRETLY HIDDEN
. . .FROM HIS WIFE

Accompanied by his nephew, an 82-year-old man came to see me in a Washington, DC suburb on an April day.

As soon as he was seated, he said, "I've got a problem."

"Oh," I said.

"Yeah," he continued, "my wife left me."

"I'm sorry to hear that. When was this?"

"Twenty-six years ago."

Surprised, I asked, "What, exactly, is the problem?"

"I never bothered to get a divorce. We are still legally married."

"Okay," I noted, "so, how is that a problem?"

"I've done pretty well in the stock market over the years. I have about $2 million in stocks and bonds ... and I don't want her to get any of it. I want my nephew, here, to get it."

In his residential state, the law says that a widow can claim a Widow's Election, about one-third of the estate. He did have a problem.

To solve the problem, I showed him how to place the assets into trusts so that there would be no probatable estate ... and no place for her to look for the Widow's Election.

One of the great features of trusts is that they can be much more private than can be a probated will.

By using a trust, you can completely foil the Widow's Election in some states. In others, the results are, in effect, the same because the trust is a quiet instrument. With no open and public probate, the other spouse is not likely to know of the estate's value.

In addition, the preferred heir will have the assets in hand ... and, perhaps, out of the country before the other spouse can begin any legal action.

A very relieved and happy pair of men left the room that April day ... and went out to enjoy the cherry blossoms.

USING THE LAST INSULT:
LIBELING ENEMIES IN YOUR WILL

From time to time, we hear of someone who uses his or her will to insult an opponent or foe. When this estate planning device is used, the planner may feel that the insult in the will is the last or only way that he can "get back" at some person.

For example, a planner might decide to insult one of his would-be heirs by writing words like these:

"I leave one dollar and my hope for a life full of misery and pain to my worthless brother, Good-For-Not-Much, who stole the inheritance that I should have received from my grandfather."

Hoping for a Hollywood-like scene, where all the family gathers in the attorney's office for the reading of the will, the planner writes the insult in the will. He assumes that all the family will hear the derogation and appreciate and understand the pain the brother caused the deceased.

This is a self-defeating strategy.

If Good-For-Not-Much decides to sue against the estate for libel ... and if he wins the case and is awarded a settlement, the planner's worst fears may be realized.

The hated family member may wind up with a substantial portion of the estate.

Our advice for using the will as a means of casting a last insult is quite simple.

Don't do it.

FUN QUIZ

CHAPTERS ONE THROUGH THIRTEEN

1. T F The "Widow's Election" refers to the increased number of women in the United States Senate.

2. T F If you die without a will, the state may "write" your will for you.

3. T F Capital gains is paid only in cities that are state capitols.

4. T F Planning to disclaim constitutes a poor plan.

5. T F For a premarital agreement to be valid, only one lawyer should be involved.

6. T F "Per Stirpes" comes into play only if your children predecease you.

7. T F "Bonding" an executor refers to his social relationship with the probate judge.

8. T F Shrinking the estate can save taxes.

9. T F The same money can be subjected to federal estate tax more than once.

10. T F Gifts placed into a "Uniform Gifts to Minors Act" account can be held until the minor attains the age of 35 years.

Test answers are shown on Page 224.

CHAPTER FOURTEEN

TWELVE STEPS TO YOUR CUSTOMIZED ESTATE PLAN

Now that you have read most of this book, you have a good idea of the great number of options you have in developing your estate plan. By now, I am sure that you have decided on some of the alternatives that you want included in your plan.

Where do you go from here?

Not to your lawyer!

Not yet, anyway.

Follow these simple steps and you will have an estate plan that is better than ninety-nine percent of all the plans in America. You will have a top-one-percent plan.

1. Re-read the portions of this book that caught your eye.

Note the pages that particularly impressed you and jot down, in some shorthand manner, the stories that etched themselves into your mind. Particular stories inscribed themselves into your mind for a reason. Subliminally, emotionally, rationally ... or in some combination of all of these, we hold on to certain information and our brain stores it for later use.

Honor your body/brain as it retains information for your brain's digestion and for continued re-processing.

2. Decide on your estate planning goals.

In order to plan your estate, you need to decide which goals are important to you. Note that I did not say that you need to decide "which tactics" are important to you. Neither did I say "which documents" you need.

Don't get ahead of yourself. Before deciding on documents, tactics and strategies, carefully delineate your goals.

To help you make some choices, use The Recer Check List for Estate Plan Goal Setting, as a means of targeting your priorities.

This form will help you to specify which goals you are seeking. Here is where you are on your own. While I have been able to offer you many ideas for possible inclusion in your plan, only *you* know what is important to you. The Check List can present some options; but only you can decide what is important to you.

I suggest that you read over the entire Check List, perhaps a couple of times. Then, put the Check List aside for a day.

Come back to it the next day and fill it out.

To help you assign a priority rating to each goal, I suggest you assign a value to each goal on a scale of one to ten.

1 = no importance

10 = absolute importance

THE RECER CHECK LIST
FOR ESTATE PLAN GOAL SETTING

_____1. Avoid probate

_____2. Avoid estate taxes

_____3. Provide for children of previous marriage

_____4. Plan for my possible disability

_____5. Provide for charitable causes

_____6. Disinherit a natural heir

_____7. Make gifts to people during my life

_____8. Provide for a person who needs special help

_____9. Protect heirs from losing their inheritance

_____10. Protect heirs from spendthrift tendencies

_____11. Protect myself against greedy heirs

_____12. Avoid income tax on my capital gains

_____13. Provide for a grandchild

_____14. Avoid excessive estate planning costs

_____15. Move personal items to certain heirs

_____16. Create more income from my assets

_____17. Keep my affairs secret

_____18. Protect my estate against publicity

_____19. Save my heirs the time and labor of probate

_____20. Get my parents' affairs in order

_____21. Provide guardians for children

_____22. Avoid family quarrels over the estate

I suggest that you write down the goals that you listed as being of prime importance. List those you assigned a score of ten.

Keeping your "tens" in mind as your primary goals, list those that you gave an "eight" or a "nine."

Read all your listed goals again and decide if you are satisfied that these really are the ones that are most important to you.

With these goals clearly in mind, you are ready to progress to the next step.

3. Decide on your choices for guardians, trustees, executors, powers of attorney and medical powers of attorney.

These are important decisions. Unfortunately, these are the decisions that often prevent people from having any estate plan whatsoever. Many are the people who have told me they cannot proceed with their estate plan because they simply cannot decide on the correct person to fill these kinds of offices.

Make it easy on yourself.

Appoint your bank or stockbrokerage trust department to fill some of the above offices. For executor, trustee and business power of attorney, your trust department is an excellent choice.

Of course, you will want a loved one to serve as your medical power of attorney. If you have minor children, you will also want a loved one to serve as guardian. Other than those offices, though, I believe you are far better served by a corporate trustee.

Do *not* choose your lawyer. Do *not* choose your accountant. If you choose one of them, he or she must serve in an individual capacity ... and you want the experience, perpetuity and dependability of a trust department. You don't want to find that a human being is on a six-week vacation in Europe when needed to serve. The trust departments don't take vacations.

4. Take all the tests in this book. Probably, you have taken the test at the end of each chapter. Take all of them again. These tests are reprinted, along with the correct answer in the Appendix. Score yourself to see how much you know. I think you will be pleasantly

surprised at the progress you have made since making the decision to read this book.

If you don't score well, re-read the portions of this book that will help you master the subjects that you have not yet tamed.

5. Diagram all of your plans.

Using the diagrammatic graphics shown in this book as a pattern, diagram your own estate plan using simple boxes on a page.

Refer to the graphics in Chapter Three.

By using this technique, you will be able to determine the correct interrelationships of the documents and to choose the correct strategies that shape the documents into a comprehensive plan.

6. Go over the diagram with your accountant, insurance professional, trust officer or private banker.

After you design your diagram, it will be helpful for you to explain it to someone else. Explain it to any one or all of the above-listed people. Tell them why you chose each document and strategy. Then ask for their input.

Remember, they are *not* expert estate planners. By the time you have read this book, very likely, you will know more than they about this subject. They *do* have experience and professional expertise that may be valuable to you. You want all the help you can get; help that can sharpen your plan.

When soliciting advice from people like this, be sure you understand exactly when they are giving you technical advice, on the one hand ... and when they are giving you personal opinion, on the other hand.

If an accountant says, "You get a partial income tax deduction for transfers to charitable trusts," he is giving you technical advice.

If he says, "My cousin invested in that company and he is not very bright; so you shouldn't invest in the stock," he is giving you personal opinion.

You certainly want the technical advice that professionals can give you but only you can determine if you want their personal opinions; I cannot help you on that score.

204

Be aware that every insurance professional has been trained to think that "insurance is the only answer to estate planning." Explain your plan to the insurance professional and get his or her input. Do *not*, I repeat, do *not* agree to purchase any life insurance product at this time.

The purpose of showing your plan to these people is to get their additional ideas and to let you size them up to see how much you can count on them for additional help when you need it.

7. Make any needed changes or refinements in your estate planning diagram.

After meeting with your advisors, you may want to revise your diagram. Perhaps you will want to start from scratch to be sure you put in both your original good ideas ... and the additional ideas your received from your advisors.

8. Make an appointment with a lawyer who is an estate planning specialist.

If you have a personal lawyer who is not experienced in estate planning, tell him that you want him to accompany you to an estate planning specialist. Go over your diagram with him prior to meeting with the specialist. Get his input.

Take the accountant and generalist lawyer with you to meet with the estate planning specialist lawyer. Tell the lawyer what you want and get him to give you an estimate of the cost for drafting the documents you have decided upon.

You may ask, "Why do I want to be paying all those people at one time?" You may think it better to just get the plan done and then go around and get their thinking.

Far better to pay each of these professionals for a few hours of their time now than to wind up with a plan like so many I have seen. Scores of people have shown me plans that were quickly drafted and that did not, in any way, reflect their desires. As far as they were concerned, they wasted every dime they put into the process.

9. After the documents are drafted, take your accountant and generalist lawyer with you to hear the specialist lawyer describe how he has carried out your instructions.

When he describes the documents, be sure you understand each phrase and clause. If he doesn't explain each item and document in Plain English, ask one of the other advisers to explain it. If it doesn't do what you want done, insist that it be changed.

10. When you are satisfied that you have the requisite documents and strategies in place, execute the documents by signing them in the lawyer's office and under his instructions.

Legion are the stories of unsigned documents left by well-intended people who "just never got around" to signing them.

11. Fund any trusts that you intended for immediate funding.

If you created a Living Revocable Trust, transfer assets to it. You may want your attorney and accountant to help you be sure that you have titled each asset in exactly the correct way.

If you have created a Safety Net Trust and intend to begin funding it immediately, transfer some assets to it now.

By following a regimen similar to this one, your plan will be a winner. You will have learned all you can learn and you will have appropriately used the technical expertise of people who have much to offer.

If, at any time, you think you are being ill-served, stop the process. Stop!

Start it all over again with new advisors.

While writing this section, I was interrupted by a phone call from a Louisiana woman who wanted advice about challenging her uncle's codicil. She felt the attorney she selected was merely "giving in" to the other side.

Her question to me was, "Should I get another attorney?"

My response was this: "I cannot tell you about the qualifications of any particular professional; but if you do not feel completely comfortable with any professional you have engaged, call him up and ask what you owe him to date. Pay him and go look for someone else."

People should never work with any professional in whom they lack confidence; no professional, worth his salt, would be interested in working for anyone who did not have complete confidence in him.

12. Congratulate yourself on a job well done. If you have stayed with me throughout this book ... and have absorbed the majority of my ideas, you deserve an "At-a-person." Give yourself the credit you deserve.

EPILOGUE

If you are determined to control the disposition of your estate ... to be sure that it goes to the persons and causes that you value ... and to be sure that no unwanted person or cause receives the benefit of your life's work, you must invest considerable time and effort.

No one else will clothe you with the determination needed to learn these skills. You must engender the resolution yourself. You may need to give yourself a pep talk. To tell yourself you really can do it.

I believe you can. I know you can.

As much as I wish that I could give you a one-page set of estate planning directions, the fact is this discipline is not that simple.

Presenting a seminar in the Garden City, New York area recently, I was a little surprised when one of the three hundred attendees complained about my performance.

He said, "I came to the seminar thinking that Dr. Recer would go down the list and plan our estates."

He continued, "I didn't expect to go away with so many options."

I suppose this man thought that every person in the room had the same estate planning needs and that I would write the universal prescription on the blackboard.

Like anything that has great value in our lives, estate planning is somewhat complex. But you do not need the combined education and experience of a rocket scientist and a brain surgeon to learn how to direct an attorney to plan your estate.

Aiming for brevity, I have intentionally tried to explain your options within the bounds of a short book; but you will need to learn a good deal ... and take some of that knowledge with you to a good estate planning attorney who can carry out your wishes.

I know that you would not have purchased the book if you were not interested in benefiting from it.

Why do I know this?

Because I have made a diligent effort to listen to the people I have counseled for the past twenty years ... and in that process, I have perceived their desire to learn.

All of them came to the estate planning table in the same general manner you have come.

I hope and trust that this book will be an active learning tool in your personal life; that it will empower you to plan pro-actively and effectively. It is intended to be a tool to arm you for effective estate planning.

- J. Dan Recer

APPENDIX 1

ANSWERS TO
THE

TEST QUIZZES

CHAPTER ONE

1. T F When children divorce, the judge always returns gifted property back to the parents who gave it.

2. T F Joint ownership with right of survivorship means "if one dies, the other owns the property."

3. T F Money in a joint bank account belongs to the survivor.

4. T F A family member's death usually brings out the best in the family and the in-laws.

5. T F Stock can be held in a joint account.

CHAPTERS ONE THROUGH TWO

1. T <u>F</u>   It is impossible to disinherit an in-law.

2. <u>T</u> F   A good estate plan can benefit more than one generation.

3. T <u>F</u>   A Safety Net Trust is used only by circus performers.

4. <u>T</u> F   Probate can be avoided.

5. <u>T</u> F   A trust might, eventually, benefit unborn heirs.

CHAPTERS ONE THROUGH THREE

1. T <u>F</u> GSTT refers to a great rock entertainment group.

2. <u>T</u> F A person can make a gift to a trust.

3. <u>T</u> F A Safety Net Trust can benefit children.

4. <u>T</u> F The annual exclusion from taxes can be used every year that the donor lives.

5. <u>T</u> F An important office of a trust is that of trustee.

6. T <u>F</u> The Bypass trust is used by single people.

7. <u>T</u> F The General Partner of a Partnership can be the Trustee of a Trust.

8. <u>T</u> F A QTIP provides income to the surviving spouse.

9. T <u>F</u> It would be smart to shrink an estate of $100,000.

10. T <u>F</u> The Living Revocable Trust is created at the death of the first-to-die spouse.

215

1. <u>T</u> F   The GSTT exemption is $1 million.

2. T <u>F</u>   A trustee can legally do exactly as he pleases.

3. <u>T</u> F   Daughters can be "beneficiaries with right of survivorship."

4. T <u>F</u>   A person's annual exclusion can be used every year for 22 years after his death.

5. T <u>F</u>   At death of the farm couple, assets pass from the Safety Net Trust into the Bypass Trust.

6. <u>T</u> F   The Bypass trust can be used only by a married person.

7. T <u>F</u>   With 8 grandchildren, the farmer can use his lifetime exemption 8 times each year.

8. T <u>F</u>   A QTIP provides income to the directly IRS during the life of the surviving spouse.

9. <u>T</u> F   A trustee owns assets "for benefit of" others.

10. <u>T</u> F   The Living Revocable Trust saves probate fees.

CHAPTERS ONE THROUGH FIVE

1. T <u>F</u> The GSTT exemption and the FET exemption are identical amounts.

2. <u>T</u> F A trustee works FBO others.

3. T <u>F</u> Daughters can be beneficiaries for only 22 years.

4. <u>T</u> F Each partner in a marriage has an annual exclusion of $10,000.

5. <u>T</u> F When funding the Bypass Trust, we pay "all the tax that will ever be due" on any amount up to the lifetime exemption figure.

6. T <u>F</u> At death of the surviving spouse, both a Bypass and a QTIP Trust can be created.

7. <u>T</u> F With 8 grandchildren, the farmer can use his annual exclusion 8 times each year.

8. T <u>F</u> One can use the generation skip to skip as many as 22 generations.

9. <u>T</u> F The Safety Net Trust can be partially funded during life and partially funded at death.

10. <u>T</u> F The Pour-Over Will moves assets into the Living Revocable Trust at death of the Trustor.

CHAPTERS ONE THROUGH SIX

1. T _F_   The "three secret words" of estate planning are, "We want ours."

2. _T_ F   If the trust says that benefits are "not assignable," the trustee cannot give a beneficiary's money to anyone else.

3. _T_ F   To use the Bypass Trust most effectively, each married partner should own part of the estate.

4. _T_ F   A trust can benefit a class of people.

5. _T_ F   At death of the surviving parent, assets pass from the Bypass Trust into the Safety Net Trust.

6. T _F_   The Bypass trust can be funded with the GSTT exemption amount.

7. T _F_   With 8 grandchildren, the farmer can use his GSTT exemption 8 times.

8. _T_ F   Income from a QTIP Trust is subject to income tax.

9. _T_ F   A trustee owns assets "for benefit of" others.

10. T _F_   If one has a Living Revocable Trust, he doesn't need a will.

CHAPTERS ONE THROUGH SEVEN

1. T <u>F</u> The IRS pays a high interest rate on withheld taxes.

2. <u>T</u> F Shrinking the estate can save taxes.

3. <u>T</u> F The $600,000 lifetime exemption can be used during life or at death.

4. <u>T</u> F The annual exclusion from gift taxes is $10,000.

5. T <u>F</u> IRS agents are severely disciplined for being rude or abusive to taxpayers.

6. T <u>F</u> A Limited Partner is one who has equal voting rights.

7. <u>T</u> F A Crummey Trust "ain't so crummy."

8. T <u>F</u> "With right of survivorship" refers to living 100 years.

9. T <u>F</u> Ninety-one is a good age for a multi-millionaire to begin makingannual exclusion gifts.

10. T <u>F</u> Only checks made out to the IRS qualify as annual exclusion gifts.

1. T <u>F</u>   When one has a Living Revocable Trust, he must file a separate federal income tax return for the trust.

2. <u>T</u> F   An irrevocable trust is a taxpayer.

3. T <u>F</u>   Capital gains tax is a form of estate tax.

4. <u>T</u> F   Probate has been known to last many years.

5. T <u>F</u>   Generation skipping saves income tax.

6. <u>T</u> F   Capital gains tax is owed when one realizes a gain.

7. <u>T</u> F   Some states impose a state estate tax.

8. <u>T</u> F   If you have living great-grandchildren, you might do a double generation skip.

9. <u>T</u> F   The same money can be subjected to federal estate tax more than once.

10. <u>T</u> F   If a person lives for only the first six months of the year and earns income while living, his income is subject to income tax.

CHAPTERS ONE THROUGH NINE

1. <u>T</u> F   Most attorneys are paid by the hour.

2. T <u>F</u>   Transferring assets to children never creates a taxable event.

3. <u>T</u> F   The $600,000 lifetime exemption can be used during life.

4. T <u>F</u>   The annual exclusion from taxes is $600,000.

5. T <u>F</u>   When children divorce, the judge always returns gifted property back to the parents who gave it.

6. T <u>F</u>   Purchasing life insurance saves taxes.

7. T <u>F</u>   A tax credit can be claimed only on a Visa card.

8. T <u>F</u>   The three secret words of estate planning are, "Show me money."

9. <u>T</u> F   The Safety Net Trust can benefit grandchildren.

10. <u>T</u> F   If you like, you can create a trust to benefit IRS agents.

CHAPTERS ONE THROUGH TEN

1. <u>T</u> F   Probate is a public process.

2. <u>T</u> F   Probate can last for five years.

3. <u>T</u> F   Those who advocate the probate process have as their best advertisement that "it isn't so bad."

4. T <u>F</u>   Probate is always completed in 30 days time.

5. <u>T</u> F   Assets in a Living Revocable Trust avoid probate.

6. <u>T</u> F   Avoiding probate does not automatically mean that one avoids estate tax.

7. <u>T</u> F   Probate "ain't so bad" in the State of Delusion.

8. <u>T</u> F   Both the lawyer and the executor can claim a fee.

9. <u>T</u> F   Assets transferred to a Safety Net Trust during life do not go through probate.

10. <u>T</u> F   Proceeds of a life insurance policy, payable to a named beneficiary, do not go through probate.

CHAPTERS ONE THROUGH TWELVE

1. T **F**   When one has a Living Revocable Trust,
        he must place his IRA into it.

2. **T** F   If an irrevocable trust pays income to heirs,
        they, not the trust, pay the income tax.

3. T **F**   When you write a will, you must record it at
        the courthouse.

4. **T** F   A charitable trust can pay you income for life.

5. T **F**   The Executor or Trustee writes a big check to the
        IRS when he funds the Bypass Trust.

6. T **F**   Capital gains tax is owed when one inherits property.

7. **T** F   Some states impose a state inheritance tax.

8. T **F**   A Limited Partner manages the partnership.

9. T **F**   A "consecutive life estate" refers to a prison term.

10. **T** F   A "Last-to-die" insurance policy pays only when both
        of the insured people die.

CHAPTERS ONE THROUGH THIRTEEN

1. T <u>F</u> The "Widow's Election" refers to the increased number of women in the United States Senate.

2. <u>T</u> F If you die without a will, the state may "write" your will for you.

3. T <u>F</u> Capital gains is paid only in cities that are state capitols.

4. <u>T</u> F Planning to disclaim constitutes a poor plan.

5. T <u>F</u> For a premarital agreement to be valid, only one lawyer should be involved.

6. <u>T</u> F "Per Stirpes" comes into play only if your children predecease you.

7. T <u>F</u> "Bonding" an executor refers to his social relationship with the probate judge.

8. <u>T</u> F Shrinking the estate can save taxes.

9. <u>T</u> F The same money can be subjected to federal estate tax more than once.

10. T <u>F</u> Gifts placed into a "Uniform Gifts to Minors Act" account can be held until the minor attains the age of 35 years.

APPENDIX 2

NEW LEGISLATION

1997 LEGISLATION

Congress has recently passed a bill which increases the lifetime exemption for Federal Gift and Estate Tax from the present level of $600,000 to $1 million.

The present increases are as follows:

LIKELY LEVELS OF THE LIFETIME EXEMPTION FROM FEDERAL ESTATE AND GIFT TAX		
YEAR	LEVEL (In Thousands)	TAX SAVINGS
1998	625	$9,250
1999	650	$18,500
2000	675	$27,750
2001	675	$27,750
2002	700	$37,000
2003	700	$37,000
2004	850	$95,500
2005	950	$134,500
2006	1 million	$153,000

SOURCE: Grant Thornton   The Washington Post

APPENDIX 3

FINDING A <u>GOOD</u> . . .
. . . LAWYER

HOW TO FIND
A COMPETENT ESTATE PLANNING ATTORNEY

To implement any of the legal documents discussed in this book, you should use the services of an appropriate attorney. Do not use a lawyer unless that person is qualified in estate planning. The law is a very broad subject and no individual attorney can possibly be competent in all aspects. Be sure you are dealing with one who will create your documents properly.

Ask for referrals. Talk with financial professionals such as bank trust officers, CPAs, stock brokers, financial planners. These people in the financial world often know who the good estate planning attorneys are. You can also go to the library and refer to the Martindale-Hubble directories. These list all the law firms in the United States. Find the directory covering your state and your area. Under the firm's listing and names of the partners you'll see listed the specialties of the firm. In some few cases they will say they specialize in estate planning.

From the Martindale-Hubble directory and local professionals, you'll get some suggested firms. If you live in a small town or rural area, you may have to search in a larger city.

If you've heard the same names mentioned several times, call them on the phone. You can't measure their degree of competency over the phone but you can get a sense of the person and if they sound like someone you want to deal with. Also ask them to tell you about their fees. You are buying something and have a right to know the price, at least approximately. The fees for legal work are not standard. They can be in a wide range. If you are then still interested, you can ask for a brief consultation...15 or 20 minutes. This should be at no charge. Its purpose is for you to get a better sense of his credentials and of him as a person: does he listen and explain things to you so that you can easily understand.

Through this searching and qualifying process you should locate someone who will perform well, whose fees are reasonable and with whom you are comfortable.

INDEX

Income Tax
  capital gains, 94
  deduction, 132, 153
  federal, 86
  life insurance and, 156
  retirement plan and, 165
  Safety Net Trust and, 50, 97
  tipping the IRS, 75
Insurance agents, 82, 110,
Inter vivos trusts. *See* Living trusts
Intestate, 172
IRA, 86, 165
Irrevocable Trust
  avoid asset loss, 64
  intended beneficiary, 69, 191
  Safety Net Trust, 97
  trustee for, 192

J
Joint Tenants with Right of
  Survivorship - JTWROS
  or JTROS, 5, 14, 23

L
Last Will and Testament,
  See Wills
Life Estate Deed
  probate and, 116
  Safety Net Trust and, 139-140
  who needs it, 158
Life Insurance, 82, 110, 116, 166, 205
  who needs it, 154
Life Insurance Trust - LIT, 156
Lifetime Exemption
  Bypass Trust and, 38, 148, 188
  federal estate tax and, 49
  QTIP Trust and, 40
  tax avoidance procedure, 88-90, 98
  unified credit, 87
  used during life, 178-180, 182
  using properly, 77
  value, 99
Limited partnerships, 60,81,175
  annual exclusion gift, 77
  Crummey Trust, 46

Safety Net Trust and, 44, 49
trustee's shares, 48
voting powers, 26
who needs it, 168
Living Revocable Trusts - LRT
  Bypass Trust and, 38, 148
  IRA and, 165
  IRS and, 97
  power of attorney and, 161
  probate and, 21, 25, 103-105,
  124, 147
  QTIP and, 149
  Safety Net Trust and, 41
  transfer assets to, 23
  trustee(s), 26
Living Irrevocable Trusts
  avoid losing assets with, 64-65, 69
  income tax on, 97
  Safety Net Trust, 29, 66, 191
  trustee for, 192
Living Wills
  as part of an estate plan, 23, 59
  medical power of attorney and,
  25- 26, 161

M
Marital estate
  assets in, 64
  premarital agreements, 190, 191
  Safety Net Trust and, 72
Marriages, subsequent
  children by, 9, 158
  joint and concurrent life estate, 159
Medical Directive. *See* Living Will
Medical Powers of Attorney -
  MPOA, 234
Move clause, 192

N
Net estate. *See* Taxable estate
"Not Assignable", 37-38, 60, 71-72

O
"Only My Issue", 31, 63, 69